Levine, Beth

AUTHOR

Divorce: young people
TITLE   Issues
Caught in the middle In Focus

DATE DUE	BORROWER'S NAME

DIVORCE

Young People Caught in the Middle

—Issues in Focus—

Beth Levine

ENSLOW PUBLISHERS, INC.
44 Fadem Road   P.O. Box 38
Box 699   Aldershot
Springfield, N.J. 07081   Hants GU12 6BP
U.S.A.   U.K.

Dedication

My deepest thanks to my husband, Bill, who held down the fort while I wrote; to my mother (babysitter extraordinaire); and to my son, Levi, who at the age of one finally learned how to nap twice a day!

Library of Congress Cataloging-in-Publication Data

Levine, Beth.
    Divorce: young people caught in the middle / Beth Levine.
      p. cm. — (Issues in focus)
    Includes bibliographical references and index.
    ISBN 0-89490-633-X
    1. Divorce—United States—Juvenile literature. 2. Children of divorced parents—United States—Juvenile literature. [1. Divorce.] I. Title. II. Series: Issues in focus (Springfield, N.J.)
HQ834.L473 1995
306.89—dc20   94-33430
                                    CIP
                                     AC

Printed in the United States of America

10 9 8 7 6 5 4 3 2 1

Cover Illustration: Deneve Feigh Bunde, Unicorn Stock Photos

Contents

Acknowledgments

The studies and examples you will find in this book are based on the tireless efforts of researchers working in the field, and on the experiences of many young people.

In 1971, Judith Wallerstein, Ph.D., founder and director of the Center for the Family in Transition, Corte Madera, California, began the first long-term study of the effects of divorce on family members. The study began with sixty divorcing or disrupted families, which included 131 children between the ages of two and eighteen. The information she gathered in her continuing fifteen-year study became the basis for her landmark book *Second Chances* (Ticknor & Fields, 1989), written with Sandra Blakeslee. Dr. Wallerstein generously discussed her discoveries with me in two separate interviews in 1988 and 1989.

I also owe a debt of gratitude to several other authorities who either graciously consented to be interviewed by me in 1993, or whose work and helpful guidance proved invaluable:

Robert E. Emery, Ph.D., professor of psychology, University of Virginia, is the author of *Marriage, Divorce and Children's Adjustment* (Sage Publications, 1988).

Frank F. Furstenberg, Jr., professor of sociology, University of Pennsylvania, is the author of *Divided Families: What Happens to Children When Parents Part* (Harvard University Press, 1991).

Neil Kalter, Ph.D., is the director of the Center for

the Child and Family, University of Michigan, Ann Arbor. An associate professor of psychology and psychiatry at the university, he is also the author of *Growing Up with Divorce: Helping Your Child Avoid Immediate and Later Emotional Problems* (The Free Press, 1990).

Laura E. Levine, Ph.D., a clinical psychologist in Glastonbury, Connecticut, is also my beloved big sister.

Howard Pobiner is a divorce lawyer in White Plains, New York.

Silvio Silvestri, Ph.D., is the director of the Center for Adult Children of Divorce, South Lake Tahoe, California.

Howard Yekell, psychologist, is the clinical supervisor of the Open Center, Shrewsbury, New Jersey.

The young people whose stories you will read here are composites drawn from the research of these authorities and from various children of divorce whom I have observed.

For a more detailed list of my research sources, please see the Bibliography at the end of the book.

Why Read This Book?

I hope to provide you with the background you need to start forming your own opinions about how divorce affects young people. This book will explain what happens before, during, and after a divorce. It will present some theories that experts have posed concerning the development of young people whose parents have divorced. Keep in mind, however, that these are just theories. You may not agree with them as your experience might be very different. I provide them only so that you may use them for the basis of discussion with your parents, your teachers, your friends, your classmates, or your boyfriend or girlfriend. Through this, I hope that you will sort out your own feelings about divorce and come to your own conclusions. You will then be as prepared as any expert to let the world know what it means to young people when families fall apart.

1

A Tale of Two Sisters

When Jenna's father packed up his things to leave the family, the eight-year-old girl clung to his leg as he tried to go out the door. "When will you be back?" she sobbed. "Who will make your dinner?"

Her three-year-old sister Kelsey didn't understand what was happening, and so was spared the emotional upset. "Bye-bye, Daddy," she waved happily, and then went back to her toys.

Their father, who had been having an affair during the marriage, never did move back. After a quick divorce, he married the other woman. The girls' mother was devastated; Jenna became her confidante and ally. "I was the one who stayed up nights with Mom while she screamed and cried about Dad," she said, "I also took care of Kelsey a lot during that time because Mom just couldn't get it together."

Kelsey was a funny, relaxed little girl who, over the years, continued to take all the emotional upheaval and commotion in stride. "The divorce just didn't seem as big a deal to me as it did to Jenna," she said, now age twenty-four. "But then, I don't remember the time when Dad was home like Jenna does."

After a few years, their mother got her life back together. She found a good job at a local bank and discovered that she enjoyed the working life. She developed her interest in singing by joining a local choir where she found quite a few friends. She never did remarry, but she seemed content with her life and gave the girls a good home.

But Jenna and Kelsey grew up to be two very different people. Jenna never lost her anger at her father or the feeling that the world was a scary, unpredictable place. She stuck close to her mother and forfeited college in order to stay nearby. Today, at age twenty-nine, she lives alone, drifting from one bad relationship with a man to another.

Kelsey also had a difficult time because she never got along with her stepmother and her relationship with her father was never close. "I know my stepmother fools around on Dad, but what am I supposed to do? It's not like he ever paid much attention to me so why should I be there for him?" she explained. But despite her unhappy relationship with her father and his wife, Kelsey has always managed to keep her sense of adventure and fun, and to maintain her positive outlook on life. She has made a good marriage and has started a promising career as a graphic designer.

"Yeah, Dad was a jerk. Still is, actually. And I will

always think my stepmother is a sleaze," Kelsey said, her laughter lightening her words. "But you know what? Life is too short. I've got a great husband, my dream job, a really good life, you know? I just can't be bothered getting upset with the past anymore."

Jenna and Kelsey were raised in the same family, experienced the same divorce, but each one coped with the family crisis in very different ways. Years after the event, one is still floundering while the other has made a successful transition to adulthood. Perhaps it's because of the additional stresses that Jenna endured or because she was older than Kelsey. Or perhaps it's simply due to the fact that Kelsey would be a more happy, upbeat person, regardless of her family history.

How do young people adjust to divorce? When there is this unpredictable mixture of internal and external forces at work, it is difficult to say, "This is exactly how you are going to feel. This is precisely what will happen to you." As you can see, everyone reacts differently to stresses in their lives. The aim of this book is to show the *possible* effects divorce can have on young people and why. What can it mean to kids when their families fall apart? How might it touch them emotionally, economically, physically, and spiritually? Are the effects short-term or long-term? How can we help affected young people cope?

Divorce Affects Everyone

You may think, "My parents aren't splitting up. Why should I care?" Why? Because divorce doesn't just affect kids from disrupted families; it affects all young people. First, consider these figures:

- Today, one out of two marriages is expected to end in divorce.[1]
- Every year, a million new children will see their parents split up.[2]
- It is estimated that 44 percent of children born between 1970 and 1984 will live in a single-parent home before the age of sixteen.[3]
- For children born in the 1990s, that figure could reach 60 percent.[4]
- The U.S. Bureau of the Census is projecting that in the 1990s, this will mean fully 40 percent of all children growing up in America will be in divorced families.[5]

Remarriage doesn't seem to end the process either. The Foundation for Child Development, New York City, conducted a study called the National Survey of Children. In 1976, it interviewed a random sampling of seven- to eleven-year-olds in the continental United States and then followed up on them in 1981 and 1986. Fully one third of the children who responded reported that their parents' second marriages ended by the time the children were in their teens.[6] Judith Wallerstein, Ph.D., founder and executive director of the Center for the Family in Transition, Corte Madera, California, in her landmark study of the long-term effects of divorce, found that, of her subjects, half of the children saw their father or mother get a second divorce within ten years of the first one.[7]

As you can see by these figures, divorce has a very widespread effect in this country. In fact, it has become part of the culture. Haven't you ever gone to a wedding or observed a married couple and thought, "Well, I wonder how long *that* will last?" The uncertainty of today's marriages has communicated itself to everyone.

Divorce's pervasiveness may be causing you to worry that your parents will split up some day. Or you may have to help a friend or relative whose parents are divorcing. It also affects the way you think about marriage for yourself. You may be overly concerned about making the right choices in life because you are so afraid of going through a divorce. On the positive side, your concern may stop you from making mistakes by forcing you to think through what exactly it is you want from a marriage and a mate. When you see the heartbreak that a divorce can cause, you will be less likely to jump into a questionable marriage.

"My parents are great together. I have no reason to think they're going to split," sixteen-year-old Grace said thoughtfully."But my best friend's parents just broke up, and she had absolutely no idea that it was in the works. She's just a wreck. I mean, they seemed like a perfect couple. Whenever I was there, they were always laughing and making jokes and doing stuff together."

Grace stopped and took a deep breath."It makes you wonder: Can anyone split up? How can you possibly know when you've found the right person? What if he's right for now but twenty years later, he'll be Mr. Wrong? I used to dream of meeting some guy in college and getting married as soon as we graduated. Now, I don't know. . ." her voice drifted off. "Nothing is ever certain in life, is it?"

2

Before the Divorce

Thirteen-year-old Mark sat rigidly in his seat in the back of the car as he felt the stony silence build between his parents in the front seat. The knot in his stomach told him that they were heading toward another blowout, and he prepared for the first outburst as if he were going to be physically hit. His mother wanted them to spend more time together as a family; his father preferred spending his free time with his buddies. Every once in a while his father gave in and accompanied them on another one of those forced outings that usually ended in misery. Today, they were going to a museum.

"There's an interesting exhibit on airplanes I think you and Mark will like," his mother finally offered into the tense stillness.

His father did not respond, except to flip a cigarette out the window.

"Well, aren't you going to at least say something?" his mother demanded.

"I'm here, okay? Isn't that enough?" his father snapped back.

Mark shut his eyes tightly and wished himself anywhere but there—some place where parents didn't fight, some place where parents liked each other. He thought longingly of his friend Michael, whose family seemed so close, so comfortable with each other. "Why can't my parents laugh and kid around the way Michael's do?" he thought.

The signs were there in Mark's family that his parents' marriage was going through rocky times. But tension and unhappiness in a marriage don't necessarily mean that it will end in divorce. The relationship between parents, like any relationship, is constantly evolving and changing. Just as you are not the same person you were ten years ago, your parents grow in different ways over time as well. Every marriage will go through periods of stress and strain as a couple deals with these changes. Perhaps there are outside hardships such as illness and financial problems that are causing them to rethink the way they live. Perhaps there are inner changes as each marriage partner develops different interests and opinions.

Many couples find the changes exciting, thinking that they help keep a marriage interesting. And many couples find that going through crises together makes them feel even closer to one another. Others are surprised to discover that marriage takes work; they must really think about their relationship and find ways to make it satisfying to both partners. Maybe Mark's parents

14

just needed to figure out ways to be together as a family and still be able to give his father some time alone to let off steam.

Other couples, however, get to a point where they just can't make the effort anymore. Sometimes one partner realizes he or she just doesn't love the other one. Or they both realize they have nothing in common. Jack and Louise, for example, got married when they were still in high school. After fifteen years, they discovered that they had grown in such different ways that neither had any interest in anything the other was doing. Where Louise used to think Jack's interest in fishing was fun, she soon got tired of wading into freezing water at the crack of dawn in order to be with him. She had always been interested in writing but had been too embarrassed to show anyone her work. Recently, she had taken a creative writing class and the teacher had encouraged her to submit her work to a magazine. The magazine bought a short story and asked for more. Louise was thrilled, but when Jack read her work, he didn't understand what she was writing about. He was hurt that she would rather spend time alone with a word processor than go on fishing expeditions with him.

They soon realized that although they still cared for one another, they had become strangers. Louise found more pleasure in being with the people in her class than she did with Jack, and Jack felt more relaxed being alone in nature than he did with Louise and her new friends.

There are other reasons why a marriage breaks up. Perhaps one partner is being physically violent or mentally cruel to the other. Perhaps there is a problem of alcohol or drug abuse. Or maybe one partner has simply fallen out of love with his or her spouse and in love with somebody else. The end result is that the couple can no longer see a reason to work at the relationship because the marriage no longer gives them any satisfaction, pleasure, happiness, or stability. They are forced to make the difficult decision to begin divorce proceedings.[1]

This is complicated enough when the couple is childless. Each partner gets a lawyer, and they negotiate an agreement whereby the couple divides up their property. While they are physically disentangling their lives, they must also separate emotionally. They have to relearn how to be independent of each other and accept the fact that they will no longer be husband and wife. When they do both those things—and that can be a very long process—their lives can go on from there in the separate paths that they wish to take.

A divorce can never be so final if the couple has children because of one very important fact: parents have the option of finding new spouses, but kids can't find new parents. And they don't want to. They love the parents they have. A divorcing couple, even if they both remarry, will always be linked together by their children.

Just a few decades ago, couples who were unhappy with each other remained married "for the sake of the children." They felt it was better for the children to have two parents in the home, even if they disliked each other, than for the children to have to deal with a "broken" home. Experts today don't believe that is so. Robert Emery, Ph.D., of the University of Virginia, has reported that children in conflict-free, divorced homes have fewer behavior problems than children who live with parents who are unhappily married.[2]

Living in a War Zone

Divorce is a process. Parents don't just wake up one day and decide to end a marriage. The problems surface long before the final split takes place. A couple will usually take years before agreeing to break up. In one study of divorced couples, half of the women reported that they had thought about separating for at least two years before doing so.[3]

What does it feel like to live with parents who are building up to a divorce? Unfortunately, no matter how discreet a couple is about their fights or unhappiness, most young people can't help but pick up on what is happening in their homes. In the National Survey of Children, 56 percent of the divorced couples whose children were included in the survey reported fighting frequently before breaking up. More than a third of those admitted that the fights sometimes became physically violent. When the violence occurred, children were witnesses two thirds of the time.[4] These young people are truly living in an emotional and sometimes physical war zone. How do they handle it? Typically, they start to feel and wonder about many things. Some emotions they may experience are discussed on the following pages.

Anger

"Jessica, tell your father that if he doesn't come help me fix the car, he can forget about that film tonight!" Jessica's mother's face contorted with rage.

Jessica, sixteen years old, felt her pulse race. She had a major chemistry exam the next day and really needed to study. Her mother knew that, and yet here she was, standing in the doorway to Jessica's room ready to explode.

Jessica felt caught. If she refused to do as her mother said, she knew she'd be stuck for another hour while her mother complained to her about how "useless" her father was. If she complied, she'd lose another hour as she got stuck in the middle of another one of their endless arguments. "Tell your mother. . ." "Tell your father. . ." Back and forth. It never ended.

Jessica was angry. Furious, in fact. She couldn't believe that two grown people—people she was supposed to depend on—could behave so stupidly. Couldn't they see what they were doing to her? How unbelievably childish they were being?

When parents become very unhappy with each other, they sometimes lose the ability to see beyond themselves. When they are swept up in their disagreements with each other, they often can't control their emotions. Sometimes they are so upset, they drag their offspring into the fray and expect them to take sides.

Young people thrust into this situation often feel a great deal of anger. They are angry that their parents are behaving so badly, and even angrier that they expect them to get involved. But most of all, they are furious that the two people who are supposed to love them and take care of them are destroying their family and security.

Shame

Sometimes the stresses that lead to a divorce can be very difficult for young people to cope with and can make them feel ashamed of their parents. Tracy's mother, for example, was an alcoholic. Once, her mother had been arrested for driving the wrong way up an entrance ramp to the highway, and the incident made all the local papers. Tracy, thirteen years old, was so mortified, she stopped bringing friends home. Some of her friends had been forbidden to go over to her house anyway since the time her mother came to parents' night at school and passed out on a desk.

Tracy was ashamed of her mother, and she was ashamed of herself for being ashamed of her mother. She did love her but, at the same time, wished she were somebody else's daughter.

It is hard enough for young people to deal with parents who are not getting along, but when the behavior of one or both is also inappropriate, the result is extremely stressful. Let's say a parent is an alcoholic, drug addict, or gambler. Or maybe a couple pitches vicious, violent fights in public. In any case, their children can become very ashamed of their parents. That feeling is confusing and upsetting to them. How can they love their parents and wish they would go away at the same time?[5]

For teenagers, the "problem" parent can be especially difficult. This is an age when acceptance by peers is most important. When a parent's actions cause them to be ridiculed or scorned by their friends, they feel torn and distressed. They want to stick up for the parent, and, on the other hand, they are embarrassed to be seen with him or her.

Guilt

"Look at Jeff's grades! What kind of mother are you? How could you let this happen?" Jeff's father was shaking

Jeff's report card in his mother's face. "I can't be everywhere! I trust you to make sure he gets his work done!"

Jeff's mother began to cry. "I tried! I can't force him to make better grades!"

Jeff, fourteen years old, tried to intervene. His parents were fighting again, and, as usual it was all his fault. "Stop it, Dad!" Jeff yelled. "I swear, I'll do better next time!"

Jeff felt that he was responsible for his parents' troubles. Lately, they seemed to fight all the time, and it always seemed to be about him. He broke curfew. His grades were bad. He didn't keep his room clean enough. He tried to be good but it didn't seem to help. There was always something he was doing wrong. If only he could figure out how to be the son they wanted, then everything would be okay. They'd stop fighting and his father wouldn't leave them.

Many young people make the mistake of blaming themselves for their parent's problems. They think if only they could be good enough or pretty enough or smart enough or lovable enough, their parents wouldn't be so angry all the time. They feel guilty because they aren't perfect children.[6]

Indeed, the truth may be that the children aren't behaving well. They may be acting out of anger or fear. But the behavioral problems are usually the result of the parents' marital distress, not the cause.[7] Children do not have the power to split up a couple who still love and are firmly committed to each other. Conversely, they also do not have the power to keep parents together if they have stopped loving each other. If the marriage is over, it's over.[8]

"It may be partially true that the parents disagree about parenting or about what to do to solve problems that a kid has, but it is never, never, never the kid's fault that the parents are getting divorced," explained Howard Pobiner, a White Plains, New York, divorce lawyer. "The parents might be using the child as an excuse, but the problem resides either with the parents themselves or with the environment."[9]

Fear of Abandonment

Ten-year-old Gina's parents fought all the time. Her father thought her mother talked too much; her mother considered her father "boring." Gina knew her parents were headed for a breakup. As much as her parents tried to keep it from her, she heard the late-night arguing and threats. Although Gina knew the situation was impossible, she was terrified by the thought of divorce. "What happens to me then? Where do I live? Who takes care of me?" she asked. She wondered about these things because she feared that if her parents could stop loving each other, then they could also stop loving her. She was afraid that when the inevitable split came, she'd be left alone.

Many young people develop a fear of abandonment when their parents are headed for divorce. When they are stuck in the middle of open warfare and their needs seem to be overlooked, it is easy for them to think that when both parents move on to different lives, they will be left behind. It is hard for them to understand that the love between a man and a woman is different from the love a parent feels for a child. A man can stop being a husband and a woman can stop being a wife, but parents will always be parents.

This is not to say that life won't be different after the divorce. Children may not see noncustodial parents as much, and custodial parents may be less available because they have to work more, but the children will not be abandoned. They will have a place to live and someone to take care of them. Not only will parents see to that, but the government will as well. It is illegal to abandon a child.[10]

This fear of abandonment can be particularly difficult for teenagers to tackle. Teens are at an age when they are seeking independence and are fighting to establish their own identity, separate from their parents. Paradoxically, they need their parents' help and guidance to make this tricky transition from child to adult. If they fear that support is going to be withdrawn—that their parents will leave them before they can leave their parents—adolescence can become a painful process.

Fear of the Unknown

There's an old saying that the devil you know is better than the devil you don't know. Wendy, sixteen years old, could relate to that. Her life was hell. Her father routinely beat her mother, sending her to the hospital on more than a few occasions. "I can't stand any more of this," Wendy said vehemently, her face getting red at the thought of what her father had done to her mother. And yet, Wendy dreaded that her parents would get a divorce.

How could Wendy not want out of this situation? Because her stressful home life was all that she knew.

Knowing what to expect made her feel a little bit in control of her own life. If her parents were to split, she would have no idea what would happen. She would be totally out of control. Perhaps life would be even worse. She had what is called a fear of the unknown.[11]

Wendy's mother never worked outside the home, and she never handled any of the family's finances. "How could my Mom and I manage on our own?" Wendy wondered. "Who would pay the bills? Would we have to move to a new place? Dad may be out of control but at least we have a roof over our heads."[12] The "devil" she knew—her father—felt safer at that point than the "devil" she didn't know—what life would be like without him.

Ambivalence

Unlike Wendy, fifteen-year-old Jim was ambivalent about his parents splitting up. Feeling ambivalent means to experience two conflicting emotions at once. For example, Jim wanted his parents to stay together and he also wished they would split up. One part of him couldn't bear the thought of his family breaking up. He loved both parents and didn't want either one to leave. At the same time, another part of him wished they would divorce just so he wouldn't have to listen to them fight anymore.

"My parents are such idiots," Jim complained. "I'm sick of hearing them whine at each other over the stupidest things. 'Why didn't you put the soap back in the dish?' 'Why don't you ever help with the dishes?' They are like three-year-olds!"

Many young people feel torn when their parents'

23

marriage heads into trouble. On the one hand, they don't want their family to fall apart; on the other, they know if their parents divorced, the fighting would stop. Or maybe they are so angry at their parents they half-wish one or both would just go away. Young people often feel guilty about these ambivalent feelings and think, "How could I think something so horrible about people I love?" But these emotions are just normal reactions to a stressful home life.[13]

The Innocent Casualties

Undoing family ties is a long, difficult process that is bound to take its toll on the kids. It is only natural that they react with anger, fear, or sadness to the stress, uncertainty, and confusion that mark living with parents' marital strife. Children are the innocent casualties in the marriage wars.

$$\boxed{3}$$

The Divorce

As mentioned in the previous chapter, divorce is not a single event. It is a process that takes time. To many young people this comes as a shock. They think that when their parents announce their divorce, their Mom or Dad moves out, and that's the end of it. They are unprepared for the amount of physical, emotional, and legal work that has to be done.

Separation

Since divorces are covered by state law, not federal, the nature of the proceedings varies from state to state. In most cases, when a couple initiates a divorce, one party moves to a separate home. This means they live apart but are still legally married. Some couples may stay separated for the rest of their lives but never actually divorce, perhaps because of religious reasons. But even though they may live in different countries, live with another person, or never even see each other again, they cannot legally get remarried until they actually divorce.

If the couple is using the separation as a prelude to divorce, some states require that the couple separate for a specific period of time before they can be divorced. One partner moves out and sets up a separate household. Then each partner must contact a lawyer who will look out for that partner's special interests. While the divorce proceedings are being negotiated, the couple must settle on a temporary living and support arrangement. The couple establishes where they will live, who will have temporary custody of the children, and what the noncustodial parent's temporary visitation rights will be while the other aspects of the divorce are being worked out. The temporary arrangements may change once the official divorce decree is handed down; the temporary set-up allows the family members to get on with their lives while waiting for the final settlement and divorce decree.[1]

In many cases, the children will be appointed law guardians, who are lawyers obligated to protect the children's interests during the separation and, sometimes, after the divorce. Children often become a focal point on the battleground between divorcing parents. There are fights over custody, visitation rights, and child support. The law guardian is there to act as a buffer between the parents and the children, to make sure the children's rights are not trampled on. If, for example, one parent refuses the other access to the children, the law guardian steps in to handle the problem.[2]

Custody

The most important issue to children is custody. With whom will the children live and who will be allowed to make the final decisions on child-care questions? Mothers are still more likely to be awarded custody because, more often than not, both parents agree that children are better off with their mothers. The 1980 U.S. Bureau of the Census reported that 90 percent of children from disrupted families lived with their mother. Thirteen percent of young people between the ages of thirteen and fifteen lived with their fathers.[3]

There are three kinds of custody: sole legal custody, joint legal custody, and joint physical custody. In sole legal custody, the parent with whom the children live makes all the major and routine daily decisions as they bear upon the children. Often, the noncustodial parent is not consulted. In joint legal custody, although the children reside with one parent, both parents are legally responsible for them. Both parents must agree on decisions about schools, discipline, behavior, health care, and so forth. Joint physical custody means the children live alternately with one parent and then the other for specified or flexible periods of time.[4]

Once custody is established, it can be changed as children get older and their needs change. In order for it to be changed, however, parents must go back to court and work it out legally, or amend their written settlement agreement. One parent cannot arbitrarily decide to take or abdicate custodial responsibility for the children without a court order.

Usually, parents decide custody between themselves.

In a recent study, 70 percent of couples who had divorced within three years of initiating proceedings agreed on custody with little negotiating. If parents can't come to an agreement, however, it becomes what is called a contested custody case. In this case, both parents want custody so the court must decide with whom the children will be better off living.[5] The state of Michigan has passed the Child Custody Act, which stipulates what factors the court must consider before awarding custody. They are what most courts across the country generally follow as guidelines. The court must consider the following:

- The love, affection, and other emotional ties existing between the parties involved and the child.
- The capacity and disposition of the parents to give the child love, affection, and guidance, and to continue educating and raising the child in a religion and creed, if any.
- The capacity and disposition of the parties to provide the child with food, clothing, medical care, or other remedial care.
- The length of time the child has lived in a stable, satisfactory environment, and the desirability of maintaining continuity.
- The permanence, as a family unit, of the existing or proposed custodial home.
- The moral fitness of the parties.
- The mental and physical health of the parties.
- The home, school, and community record of the child.
- The reasonable preference of the child, if the court

finds the child of sufficient age to express a preference.

- The willingness and ability of each parent to facilitate and encourage a close and continuing parent-child relationship between the child and the other parent.
- Any other factor the court considers relevant to a particular child custody dispute.[6]

Why Can't Children Decide Their Own Futures?

A judge will often consult with children in his or her chambers (office) as to with which parent they wish to live. These dialogues are recorded by a court reporter but then the files are sealed. Neither the parents nor the lawyers can read what the children said. The judge takes the children's preferences into account when handing down a decision, especially if the children seem mature and articulate, but unless the children are aged approximately thirteen or over, those wishes will rarely be determinative.[7]

Stanley S. Clawar, Ph.D., a clinical sociologist and associate professor of social science at Rosemont College, Rosemont, Pennsylvania, has identified basic reasons why young people have difficulty making appropriate decisions regarding custody. He states that when pushed, children make their choices based on fears and reasons such as the following:

- Anger at one parent, whom they feel has hurt or abandoned them or the other parent.
- Fear of reprisal from the parent with whom they are spending more time.

- One parent's having turned the children against the other parent.
- Fear and guilt about leaving the unmarried parent alone.
- Confusion of values—one parent promises the children material goods.
- A need to be with the parent who the children see the least.
- Hostility rising from new stepfamily relations ("I don't want to live with my stepfather!").
- A need to rescue the parent who seems to be hurting ("My Mom will be too sad if I see more of my Dad").[8]

In making custody decisions, therefore, the court will give much more weight to the capability of the individual parents, the stability of the home life, and the question of who else will be living in the home with the children. Judges try to preserve the young people's predivorce lifestyle as much as possible. They want to establish which parent's home will present as little disruption to the children as possible. The parent who wants to stay in the same home where the children will attend the same school, be near relatives, and have the same friends will have a better chance of getting custody than the parent who wants to move the children across the country.[9]

Although many young people are angry that their lives are being decided without their input, some would just as soon not be consulted on which parent they would rather live with. As Robert E. Emery, a professor of psychology at the University of Virginia, writes in his book, *Marriage, Divorce and Children's Adjustment,* "If being caught in the middle of their parents' conflicts is one of the greatest sources of distress for children, then soliciting their opinion as to who is their preferred custodian is hardly a solution. The articulation of a preference can be tantamount to asking children to choose between their parents, a choice which is hardly a solution to their torn loyalties."[10]

Investigations in Contested Custody

If custody does become an issue, young people should be forewarned that they will have to talk to court investigators who will be looking at the arrangements made for the children in both potential homes. Either the investigator will come to the children's home or their law guardian will bring them to the investigator's office. The court investigator will ask the young people about their parents, siblings, home life, and school in order to find out about the quality of life they could expect to enjoy with each parent. Sometimes, the young people might also have to talk to a court-ordered psychiatrist who is called in to help determine who is the better parent.[11]

If young people are not prepared for these strangers in their lives, these meetings can be quite traumatic. In some cases, parents are not allowed in the meetings so their children will be alone with the law guardian, the court investigator, and the psychiatrist. In young people's eyes, these professionals can seem like scary strangers who are poking around in their very private business.

In cases where one parent accuses the other of physical or sexual child abuse, the custody hearings can become even more frightening. The young people will be brought to strange doctors who will have to examine their genitals for trauma or their bodies for bruises. The children will be asked very difficult and troubling questions that they might not be emotionally ready to answer.

"When you are dealing with cases of abuse or false claims of abuse, the children will need help in dealing with the psychological effects. But the appropriate place for that is in a nurturing therapeutic setting, not a court of law which is where, unfortunately, a lot of these cases are brought out. It can be exceedingly difficult for children," explained Howard Pobiner, a White Plains, New York, divorce lawyer.

Visitation Rights

The next order of business is working out visitation rights for the noncustodial parent: how often and under what circumstances can that parent see his or her children? Fifteen-year-old Julia, for example, stayed with her father every weekend and for two months in the summer. In cases where it has been established that the noncustodial parent has been abusive, visitation may be denied altogether or allowed only under supervised conditions.

One problem young people often run into with visitation rights is that the law does not take into account their changing needs. When Julia was five years old, she not only enjoyed seeing her father every weekend, she needed to. It was very important to her to see that her Daddy was okay. "I was afraid he was lonely," Julia recalled. "I kept thinking, 'If Mom and I aren't there, who does he talk to?' It made me feel better just to see him say hi to his neighbor."

But now Julia is a teenager, and like every adolescent she wants to start separating from her parents. She'd rather spend her Saturday nights hanging out with her friends or going on school trips than staying home with Dad. According to the law, however, she has to spend every weekend with him. Her father, who misses her terribly, won't give an inch on the subject. "I don't get to see Julia all week and soon she'll be going off to college. It may sound selfish but I don't want to have to share the little time I have with her," he said.

There are ways around this problem if the noncustodial parent can show more flexibility. Howard Pobiner recommends that the son or daughter be allowed to bring friends along on visitation. "It makes visitation into a sort of extended family trip. It is much more comfortable because the kid gets his best buddy, the father can observe the interaction and understand what the conversations are about. Plus the father doesn't have to be constantly coming up with entertainment. Generally everyone has a better time," Pobiner explained.

If one parent's situation changes after the visitation schedule has been set up—for example, one parent has accepted a job that will take him or her across the country—the former couple must renegotiate visitation rights. Obviously, their children cannot visit the noncustodial parent every weekend if one parent is in California and the other is in Florida.[12]

A noncustodial parent can also go back to court and get help if the custodial parent refuses to allow him or her access to the children as stipulated in the separation or divorce decree. The court will force the custodial parent to live up to the agreement. In extreme cases, if the custodial parent continues to refuse to grant visitation rights and cannot show just cause for doing so, the children may be taken away and custody awarded to the other parent if it is in the children's best interests. Generally, however, courts are reluctant to move young people back and forth.

Child Support

In the divorce negotiations, parents must also establish child support payments. These are monthly payments made by the noncustodial parent to the custodial one to be used for the housing, care, feeding, and clothing of the children. This is almost always the father since, in general, men still make more money than women. There are cases, however, where fathers who have been stay-at-home Dads, while the mothers worked, have been awarded custody and child support payments.

The amount of support is set by how much the paying parent can reasonably afford. In the past, the United States has been notorious for its low levels of child support awards and for the minimal enforcement of them. Currently, however, there is a national trend to protect children by establishing child support guidelines. Thirty states now have them. These guidelines are fairly rigid formulas that dictate a percentage of both parents' income that must be spent on the children. Once the rate has been set, child support payments must be made until the children reach a certain age established by each state, marry, or become self-supporting.[13]

In the past, child support levels, once established,

were rarely changed. It was often difficult to account for cost-of-living increases or for the fact that teenagers cost more than toddlers. States are now looking into changing that. New York, for example, is about to start a review process in which every three years the support payments are re–evaluated to see if they are still appropriate.[14]

Young People's Emotions During the Divorce

The period of time during which the divorce is being worked out can be extremely rocky for all family members. To many young people, no matter how badly their parents were getting along, the actual divorce comes as a complete shock. The National Survey of Children discovered that of the young people it sampled, only a third were given advanced warning of a month or more that separation or divorce proceedings were about to occur.[15]

Most young people react to the shock of divorce with anger and anxiety. Psychologists P. Lindsay Chase-Lansdale and E. Mavis Hetherington have established that young people typically enter a two-year crisis period.[16] What they need most of all to help them through this time of uncertainty and confusion is strong emotional support and a strongly defined structure to their lives. In many cases, however, they never receive what they so desperately need because their parents' attention is focused elsewhere.[17]

Earlier, this book discussed young people's fear of physical abandonment. Now they may have to handle a form of emotional abandonment. As a divorcing couple untangles their lives together, each partner must try to

35

establish a separate identity. They must achieve what Frank Furstenberg, professor of sociology at the University of Pennsylvania, calls "an emotional divorce."[18] As they struggle to reestablish themselves as single people, child rearing may temporarily (and in some cases, permanently) take a back seat to the work at hand.

Young people may find themselves becoming their parents' confidants, advisers, consolers, and caretakers. All of a sudden, roles have switched: the children are taking care of the parents and the parents are too stressed, overwhelmed, or preoccupied with their own anger to properly care for and protect their children.[19]

Many young people find this experience frightening and overwhelming because they feel as if no one is in charge anymore. Unless they have a sympathetic relative, teacher, or other adult who will take up the slack in parenting, they are—at least, emotionally—on their own. Dr. Judith Wallerstein calls this the "Overburdened Child Syndrome" and it will be discussed at length in Chapter 6.

Kids of divorcing parents must begin to deal with their big disappointment with the adults in their world. When children are very little, they think that their parents know everything and can solve every problem. As children become teenagers, they start to realize that their parents are just human and don't have all the answers. But children of divorce are forced to come to that realization much sooner and with much less guidance than children in happy, intact families. They see their stressed parents acting in ways that make them look less than invincible: fighting about money and property, complaining about each other, expecting their children to take sides, being depressed, angry, or sad, and forgetting that their children need help.[20]

Young people's reactions to learning of their parents' fallibility often range from denial to anger to depression.

Denial

Denial takes the form of reconciliation fantasies. Many kids dream that their parents will get back together, magically bringing their lives back to the way they used to be.[21] Ten-year-old Renny thought that his parents just needed time apart to think things over. He was sure that if he kept making his parents get together, they would realize that they still loved each other and would stop the divorce proceedings. When his father came to pick him up for his weekend visitation, Renny made sure that he wasn't ready. This forced his father to come into the house and talk with his mother while Renny pulled his gear together. And, in fact, it seemed to work. Those few times that his parents were together, the couple managed to be civil to one another. But what Renny didn't understand is that this was because of, and not in spite of, the fact that they were getting divorced. Since it was no longer her problem, the fact that his father traveled too much for business didn't bother his mother anymore. His father seemed happier because he no longer had to feel guilty about letting down his wife and child.

Anger

Anger during this time can take many forms. Some young people will lash out at both parents for letting them down. Eleven-year-old Angela, for example, fought constantly with her mother and refused to see her father when he came for visits. Other young people will fight with the custodial parent while idealizing the noncustodial parent. Twelve-year-old Evan lived with his father whom he saw as an unreasonable tyrant. His mother had moved three hours away and he saw her infrequently. Still, he fantasized that she was the "perfect" parent and that the only reason she didn't come more often was because his father was so awful. Other children deal with their rage by venting it on everyone except their parents. Their lives at this juncture are so uncertain, they don't dare do anything that might push their parents even further away than they already seem. They take their anger out on other kids or teachers—people who seem "safer" to antagonize because they don't hold the key to the children's security and well-being.

Depression

During the period of divorce negotiations, young people can also suffer from depression. If the parents are fighting, the children are devastated by seeing the two people they love the most rip each other apart. This is compounded when the parents try to get the children to take sides: "How can you possibly want to see your father after what he's done to us! He's no good!" The kids can feel so sad and hopeless that they withdraw from life. They may stop eating or sleeping or start doing both to excess.[22] They may have no interest in anything. Depression can become so severe that the kids have thoughts of suicide. People who suffer from depression should immediately seek help from a physician, who will help them get better. If treatment of depression isn't the first doctor's specialty, he or she can recommend another one who has more training in this area.

For many children of divorcing parents, this period of crisis, role reversal, and emotional upheaval is temporary. Once the divorce is finalized, the young people adjust to a new routine and the parents go back to being responsible and supportive. But for just as many parents and children, the crisis and upheaval can go on for years. The family never seems to settle into its new way. The next chapters explore what can happen to young people in the postdivorce family, beginning with economic effects.

4

The Economics of Divorce

Ten-year-old Jamie looked around her new room and tried not to cry in front of her mother. She knew her Mom had tried her best to find them a nice place to live, but where her room in her old house had been big and bright, this one was small with dingy paint and brown watermarks ringing the ceiling. Worst of all, she had to share it with her two "bratty" sisters.

When her parents divorced, Jamie's father agreed to pay child support since her mother's job as a cashier couldn't begin to pay the living expenses for the three of them. But her father's carpentry business had been doing badly, and he could afford only $200 a month. The only way they could all manage was if her parents sold their house and split up the proceeds. Her mother then rented an apartment in a less expensive neighborhood. Just when Jamie needed her friends and familiar routine most, she had to leave everyone behind and enroll in a different school.

Jamie turned away from her mother and forlornly reached out to pick some chipped paint off the wall. "It'll be okay, Ma," she said softly. "I'll put some pictures up."

One of the best-kept secrets about divorce is the economic impact it has on families. When a couple separates, expenses increase because two households cost more to maintain than one. But study after study shows that divorced mothers and children suffer more than fathers. Families headed by single mothers are more than three times as likely to be impoverished as those headed by a married couple. In 1990, 28 percent of all divorced women with children under the age of twenty-one were living in poverty.[1] In Dr. Judith Wallerstein's study, one out of four kids were put into a lower economic class because of divorce.[2]

In 1979, 45 percent of all families qualifying for Aid to Families with Dependent Children were separated or divorced.[3] One study found that the first year after a divorce, women with children under the age of 18 suffered an average 73 percent drop in their standard of living while divorced men experienced a 42 percent rise.[4] Some dispute those figures. The Panel Study of Income Dynamics at the University of Michigan reported that mothers of minor children experienced a 30 percent drop in their standard of living while their ex-husband's standard of living increased 10 to 15 percent.[5] No matter which figures you choose to believe, each paints a rather bleak financial picture. According to Frank Furstenberg, professor of sociology at the University of Pennsylvania, every year one million families experience a drop in income similar to what families endured in the Great Depression.[6]

Where Are the Support Payments?

There are many reasons for this difference between the economic levels of divorced men and women. At the top of the list is the poor record of fathers paying child support. As has already been discussed, it is still usually the mother who gains custody of the children. Noncustodial fathers are supposed to pay child support to help in raising the children, but consider these figures:

- Of the 9.4 million single mothers with children in the United States, almost two thirds do not receive financial support from the fathers.[7]
- According to 1990 U.S. Bureau of the Census figures, of the four million American women who are owed child support, one million are not receiving it.[8]
- Only half of the fathers who are ordered to pay child support pay the full amount, according to the U.S. Bureau of the Census.[9]

There are other reasons why divorced women and their children fare so poorly financially. One is a general social problem: women workers are still paid only two thirds what men are paid for equivalent work.[10] Another is the fact that child support agreements don't take into account that raising children becomes more expensive as they get older. Although there is now a trend to make support guidelines more adaptable, explained divorce lawyer Howard Pobiner, it used to be once you made a deal, and fixed a number, that was it. A contract was a contract. But where $200 a month may be adequate for a one-year-old, it won't begin to cover the cost of food, clothing, school, and athletic equipment for a teenager. And yet mothers and children are expected to scrape by on such an allowance.

The Effect on Young People

What is the effect of this economic fall–out on young people? The most immediate is that, to stop their slide down the economic ladder, many mothers may have to go back to work, seek public assistance, or enroll in school to retrain themselves for the work force.[11] The mother is then less available to her children for emotional support and physical care just when they need it most. A recent study found that the number of women who worked 1,000 hours per year rose from 51 percent to 73 percent after a separation.[12] The children are either placed in day care or learn quickly to fend for themselves.

Another major change is that, like Jamie's mother, 15 percent of divorced mothers are forced to move into less expensive housing during the first year following a divorce. This is fully seven times the rate of forced moves compared to those who are stably married.[13] Even after the first year, 20 percent of divorced mothers move during a given year—a third more than married women.[14]

This can be extremely stressful on young people as it happens at a time when they really need the comfort and stability that comes with the familiar environment of their family home. Jamie had been particularly upset by her parents' break–up. She was already feeling uncertain and confused by the coming of adolescence. Her body was changing rapidly, and she was upset by her jumbled emotions. But both parents were preoccupied with untangling their marriage and had little time to help her through this difficult period. Jamie took comfort in the fact that even though everything was changing all around her—her family, social pressures, her own body—she still had the security of her room. She felt safe there and spent many afternoons by herself, reading on her bed or just daydreaming. When Jamie learned that she would have to give up her safe haven, she felt as if her last prop had been taken away from her.

Moves to less desirable houses are doubly distressing if the children can see that the kids who are living with their father—stepchildren from a second marriage, perhaps—are living better than they are.[15] They feel rejected and may develop low self-esteem. Steve, thirteen years old, moved to a small apartment with his mother after his father left. His father remarried another woman and brought her two daughters to live with them. Since his stepmother made a good living as a financial officer, she and his father were able to combine incomes to provide a very nice lifestyle for themselves and the two girls. When Steve went to visit his father, it upset him to see that both girls had their own rooms, phones, and cars while he and his mother were basically living on tuna and macaroni and cheese. "It makes me think he doesn't love me as much as the girls. Like there was something really wrong with me," he said.

Limited Horizons

Reduced economic circumstances also limit young people's aspirations. The educational resources will probably not be as good as they were in the old neighborhood, and the mother will less likely be able to make up for it with what Neil Kalter, Ph.D., director of the Center for the Child and Family, University of Michigan, calls "growth-enhancing experiences." These experiences include extra music lessons; athletic activities; trips to museums, plays, zoos, or concerts; and owning a computer or encyclopedia.[16]

In addition, divorce agreements do not make provisions for the expense of attending college.[17] If a father does not wish to pay for college, even though he is perfectly capable of doing so, he is not obligated. Therefore, the full burden falls on the already struggling mother and child. For many young people in this situation, college becomes unobtainable because college admissions take a divorced father's income into account when deciding scholarships—regardless of whether or not he is willing to pay. The result is that not even half of the young people in Dr. Wallerstein's study have gone on to college. Of those that did, only 10 percent are receiving full financial help from one or both parents.[18]

Altogether, the ramifications of an economic decline can affect every area of young people's lives—emotional, physical, social—at a time when they are least able to cope with it. They feel unprotected financially, and by extension, physically, at a period in their lives when they also feel unprotected emotionally.

"Sometimes I have this fear that I'll go to sleep and when I wake up, my sisters will be gone," Jamie said. "I'll open the door to my room and there'll be nothing there—just sky and clouds. I'll be floating around, all alone."

5

Disappearing Dads

Lorna, fifteen years old, peered into the mirror. She had been up since early that morning getting ready for this day: washing her hair, picking out just the right outfit, doing her makeup. Finally, she thought she looked okay. Her father was coming to visit, and she wanted everything to be perfect.

"Mom!" she yelled. "Do you think my makeup is too much or do you think he'd want me not to wear any?"

Lorna's mother appeared in the bathroom doorway. It broke her heart to see her daughter trying so hard to please someone who let her down so often. Barely able to hide her anger at her ex-husband, she said meaningfully, "I don't know, honey. I don't know what he likes. After all, neither one of us has seen His Royal Highness in four years!"

Her father had called the week before to say that he

was going to be in the area and to suggest that they get together. "I'm going to take you out to the best restaurant in town, my Lorna Doone," he swore, using his old pet name for her. "Wear your best stuff!" They had made these plans before over the years, but at the last minute, something always came up. Either he forgot a previous engagement, or he had to go out of the country for business, or his car broke down. But this time, as the day drew near and there was no "Sorry, can't make it" phone call, Lorna dared to let herself dream that he was actually going to come.

Her father was supposed to arrive at noon; it was now eleven o'clock. Lorna shrugged in exasperation, "I'll have to go with it. I don't have time to change again." She then hurried to the kitchen where she prepared to bake her special brownies that she knew her Dad used to love.

Eleven o'clock turned into noon, which turned into one, and then turned into two. Her father was nowhere to be seen. Lorna and her mother looked uneasily at each other over the kitchen table, the plate of brownies between them. At two-thirty, Lorna could no longer hold onto the hope that he had been stuck in traffic. She put her head down on the table. "I can't believe I fell for it again!" she said softly.

Her mother got up and put her arms around the stricken girl. "I'm sorry, Lorna, I guess he's just not going to show. Like always."

Where Are the Fathers?

Lorna's experience with her father is not unique. There

is a disturbingly high percentage of divorced fathers in America who distance themselves from their children emotionally, physically, and financially. Of the young people represented in the National Survey of Children, more than 50 percent who lived with their mothers had not seen their fathers in the last year, and only 16.4 percent had contact once a week or more.[1]

Studies also show that contact between noncustodial fathers and their children lessens as time progresses. In some studies, 45 percent of noncustodial fathers saw their children once a week or more if they had been divorced for less than two years. But two to five years after the divorce, 31 percent of the fathers had not seen their children for a year or more. After five to ten years of divorce, that figure went up to 41 percent of the fathers. After ten years of divorce, 64 percent of the fathers had not seen their children for a year.[2]

Does the situation improve once the children become adults? According to a study conducted by psychologist Silvio Silvestri, Ph.D., Center for Adult Children of Divorce, South Lake Tahoe, California, 33 percent of divorced fathers had no contact at all with any of their adult children. Only 50 percent had a close relationship with at least one adult child compared to 90 percent of fathers from intact families.[3]

Wealth and education don't have as big a bearing on these statistics as you might think. One quarter of the young people in the National Survey of Children whose fathers were college graduates had not seen their fathers in the past year, compared to three fifths of the children whose fathers did not finish high school.[4]

49

"What Else Can I Buy You, Honey?"

Another unfortunate blow to the relationship between noncustodial fathers and their kids is that the quality of their time together decreases as well as the quantity. Think about this: when father and child live together, the major amount of contact is unremarkable, day-to-day activities such as reading a book together, recounting the day's adventures over dinner, helping with homework, playing ball, doing chores together, watching television in a family group. The father is also involved in the disciplining, such as making sure homework gets done, rooms get cleaned, curfews are obeyed. It's during those small, ordinary moments that father and child get to know one another better and share in each other's lives.

When a father sees his kids only periodically, however, that direct tie gets broken. The father feels he has so little contact with his children, he doesn't want to waste his time with them on boring activities. Instead of just hanging out with his kids, he'll plan extravagant trips to expensive restaurants, amusement parks, shows. Since he feels as if he has to win his children over when he sees them, every visit becomes a holiday. He'll lavish gifts on them and let the rules slide.[5] In these cases, the father is in danger of becoming more like an indulgent uncle to his children than an authority figure.[6]

Divorce lawyer Howard Pobiner noted, "One of the saddest things I see is when I go to the opera or ballet and see fathers with their kids, all dressed up, because this is the father's idea of good parenting. Visitation shouldn't always be a special event. It should be a routine part of life, time to do regular stuff. You don't have to go to the movies. Sitting in the kitchen and watching Dad make a meal that everyone shares together is much more important."

He continued, "Divorced fathers need to learn that kids need to go to wherever their Dad is living, watch him shave, see where he sleeps, so the kids will know that their father is okay. Many adults don't understand that their kids, in their own way, worry about them."[7]

Financial Abandonment

In addition to disappearing physically and emotionally, many divorced fathers also disappear when the time comes to pay the bills. Of all the divorced mothers in the United States who are entitled to child support payments, less than half receive the money as ordered by the court, one third receive only part of what they are owed, and one fourth don't get any money at all.[8]

You might think that fathers don't keep up with their support payments because they don't have the money. Perhaps they have remarried and simply can't afford to support two families. In some cases, this is true. But, as we saw in the dismal visiting record between divorced fathers and children, the father's income is not a significant factor in compliance: studies have shown that wealthy men don't have better payment records than poorer ones.[9]

If money isn't the whole story, what's the reason so many divorced fathers lose their connection to their kids?

Why Dads Disappear

Many, many divorced fathers try extremely hard to stay involved with their children. After all, according to the

U.S. Bureau of the Census, in 1992, 665,000 divorced fathers have at least one child under the age of eighteen living with them on a regular basis. The total number of children in their father's custody is 932,000.[10] And many fathers who do not have custody go to great lengths to make sure they remain a key part of their children's lives.

So with all these good intentions, why is there this rash of disappearing Dads? It's not fair to say these absent fathers don't love their children. Many give up not because they aren't interested but out of a sense of frustration, anguish, loss, and a feeling that they aren't wanted.

Some other possible reasons follow:

- There's still so much anger and hurt between the former husband and wife that every time he tries to see the kids, he has to relive all the bad times. He finds this so emotionally draining that he avoids the situation altogether.[11]
- The mother refuses to help arrange visits so the children have to do it themselves. They are not always capable of handling such responsibility.[12]
- The mother is so angry at the father that she blocks or tries to sabotage his attempts to see his children. Some fathers eventually just give up.
- The mother remarries, and the father feels he isn't needed or wanted anymore. "She's got a new father. What does she need me for?" he might think.[13]
- The father remarries, and puts all his energy and money into his new family.[14]
- The father or the mother and children move to

another town. Young people in the National Survey of Children were only half as likely to visit with their fathers every week if they lived more than an hour away from them.[15]

- Some fathers just don't know how to function as a parent outside a traditional family structure.[16] Many men get their sense of parental authority by acting as full-time protector and breadwinner. If they lose those roles, they don't know how else to be a father.[17]

- The father is awkward around children. His wife always smoothed the relationship between him and his children. When she is no longer there to help him, he doesn't know how to be with them.

- When some fathers remarry or their relationships with their children become distanced, they feel less committed to paying child support.[18]

The Consequences

Experts differ in their opinions about the effect of "disappearing dads" on young people. There are scores of different studies. Some say there are no long-term effects of absent fathers on children; others say the effect is drastic, resulting in depression, low self-esteem, and delinquent behavior. And still another body of research says it doesn't matter what the father does—as long as the relationship with the mother is good, the children will do well. But common sense must tell you that if your father willfully chooses not to be part of your life, it has got to hurt in a big way. You would have to be an extremely strong and confident person not to feel rejected, sad, or angry.

Young people with absent fathers often develop low self-esteem because they blame themselves for their father's disappearance. They feel rejected and unlovable. "Of course, he doesn't want to see me. Why would anyone want to be with someone as awful as I am?" they might think.[19]

Other young people start blaming their mother for the loss of their father. They are furious that their father has disappeared, but he isn't there to fight with. It's only natural that they might turn that anger on the parent who is there—their mother. In so doing, they often idealize their father, conveniently forgetting his bad points.[20]

Franco, sixteen years old, hadn't seen his father in eight years, but he was quick to point the finger at his mother. The reality of the situation is that his father was a compulsive gambler who abandoned the family after cleaning out their savings account. Before and after the divorce, his mother struggled to keep Franco and his brothers clothed and fed. But Franco had shut all those bad times out of his mind. According to Franco, his father was a fun guy, who always had time for his sons; it was only because his mother was such a "pain" that he left. "She was always on him about money and stuff. I know he would contact us if he didn't have to deal with her," he said bitterly. Deep down, Franco knew that his mother wasn't really to blame, but his father wasn't there to receive his wrath. Franco had no one else to vent his anger and hurt on except his mother.

The Need for a Father

Young people need their dads. It used to be thought that

a stepfather could take the place of an absent father, but experts are discovering what young people could have told them all along: that as they get older, adolescents experience a growing need to establish contact with their fathers, even if they have a solid relationship with their stepfathers.[21]

Teenage boys and teenage girls yearn for their absent fathers for different reasons.

Teenage Girls and Their Fathers

When girls enter their teenage years, they start wondering whether they are feminine and lovable.[22] Fathers provide the first confirmation that they are. Just a word from the father, such as "You look really pretty today" as the girl dashes off to school, or even "Don't let that boy treat you that way—you deserve better!" is all the girl needs to bolster her confidence in herself as a woman.

Young women need their fathers to acknowledge them, to show that they think their daughters are attractive, nice, and worthwhile. The daughters crave an overall sense of importance in their fathers' lives.[23] If the father is not in the home, the girl has to struggle to get that approval, because the father just isn't there for that day-to-day casual contact. Many young women go to great lengths to capture their fathers' attention. If the fathers are absent altogether, there is no chance that the girls will get that boost and recognition.

Teenage Boys and Their Fathers

Teenage boys have two problems when their fathers disappear. The first is that they have no role model. Boys look to their fathers to see what it is a man should be. They learn from their dads what is appropriate masculine behavior, what are good ways to use and control their feelings of aggression, and how to relate to women. When their is no male role model in their lives, boys have to figure it out for themselves.

A connected problem is that a teenage boy, left in his mother's care with no male authority figure in his life, often feels like a "mamma's boy" and starts to resent her authority.

The combination of lacking a male role model and being dependent on their mother makes many boys feel unsure of their ability to be a "man." This forces many boys to act out, in a mistaken attempt to prove they are one. They'll adopt many stereotypically aggressive male behaviors such as fighting, getting into trouble in school, driving too fast, or refusing to listen to adult authorities.[24]

What to Do?

A father's absence in the home doesn't have to be a sentence of life long unhappiness for the children. If a young person's father has "disappeared," he or she may find that seeking out another male adult, who can provide a positive relationship, may help him or her get through some tough times. Although a good relationship with a stepfather cannot fully replace a father, especially if the stepfather comes on the scene later in the young person's life, the stepfather, or another male figure such as a grandfather, uncle, teacher, or coach, can have a constructive influence on the children's lives. They may not be able to take the hurt and confusion away altogether, but they can help the children get back on track.

The truth is, however, that the "disappearing dad" is one of the saddest byproducts of divorce. It is sad for the father as well as the children for he is missing out on one of the greatest joys in life: his kids.

6

The Aftermath: How Young People Adjust Emotionally

Experts used to assume that after a divorce occurred, the family mourned, got over it, and then everyone got on with their lives. Researchers today, however, are challenging that hypothesis, but even they don't really know for sure. Much reference has been made in this book to Dr. Judith Wallerstein's fifteen-year study in which she has found that divorce does leave lasting scars. It should be noted that other experts have disagreed with her findings because the subjects included only white, middle-class families and because she didn't have a control group of young people from intact families. "Without a control group, you can't compare children's experience of divorce with the general experience of what it's like to grow up in today's society," explained Robert

Emery, Ph.D., professor of psychology at the University of Virginia in Charlottesville.[1]

Suffice it to say that the jury is still out on the definitive answer on the long-term effects of divorce. Only young people themselves will be able to tell us. With that in mind, the following two chapters will examine in general what happens to young people after their parents' divorce.

The Crisis Years

A major part of the divorce process for parents and their children takes place after the final split. Each family member must make peace with the crisis before he or she can start rebuilding a new and better life. That's a very tall order for adults, who have life experience and emotional resilience; it's that much harder for young people, who don't yet have those qualities. How do kids cope after the divorce? What stresses are they likely to encounter?

Psychologists P. Lindsay Chase-Lansdale and E. Mavis Hetherington have called the two years following a breakup the "crisis" period.[2] This time is typified as one of emotional upheaval as each family member deals with the shock.

There are two things young people need during this time of turmoil: additional emotional support and a predictable routine.[3] Sadly, these are usually the very things that depressed, anxious parents cannot provide in the crisis period.

The custodial parent, usually the mother, is overwhelmed with becoming single again, being a solo parent, putting her finances in order, and working through her anger or sadness over her divorce. She may have to go back to work or take on a second job. If she has been a full-time mother, she may need to go back to school to retrain herself for the work force. The noncustodial parent must also put his financial house in order, sort out his emotions about the divorce, figure out how to remain involved in his children's lives, and establish a new social network. The parents just aren't as available, emotionally and physically, to their children as they once were.[4]

Many young people discover that during this time of crisis the family roles may be temporarily reversed. The children find themselves taking on more responsibility around the house such as the cooking and cleaning. Older siblings will act as parental figures to younger ones. When fifteen-year-old Peter's parents split up, his mother went into a depressive state. She slept most of the day, getting up only once in a while to eat. Peter took charge of his seven-year-old twin sisters, Rebecca and Emma. He got them up for school, packed their lunches, and read them their bedtime story.

As part of the reversal, parents will lean on their children emotionally in ways they have never done before. Peter's mother, for example, needed to have her son tell her she was still pretty, that she would remarry one day, and to otherwise shore up her eroding confidence. Peter became the only one who could cajole her out of bed. "Let's take the girls to the beach," he would suggest, while opening the window shades. "Why don't you wear your white suit? You look really nice in it."

Other parents, feeling lonely, may depend on their children for companionship. In turn, these young people feel too afraid or guilty to leave that parent alone and will sacrifice many childhood experiences—playing with friends, going to movies or the mall, school trips—to stay with the anguished parent. Some young people believe (some rightly so) that they are the only ones keeping a parent from despair or suicide.

The short-term effects of a parent's "diminished capacity" on young people can be dramatic. Children can become severely depressed or anxious when they suspect that no one is in charge. They are at risk for developing behavioral and emotional problems. Teresa Peck, a clinical psychologist at the Center for the Family in Transition, Corte Madera, California, discovered a connection between poor grades and divorce. She has said, "What I've found is that 78 percent of the underachievers—kids with grade averages in the A–B range in the lower schools, who had fallen into the D–F range in high school—came from families of divorce, compared to only 30 percent of the achieving kids—those who maintained an A–B average consistently over the years."[5]

That is not to say that all is gloom and doom. There is an upside to the crisis period. Because young people must assume more responsibility, they become socially competent and mature at an earlier age than their peers. Young people enjoy and are proud of being treated as an adult. Parents, however, must be vigilant about not making so many demands that their children have no other life outside of the responsibilities of their home.

The Long-Term Prognosis

Divorce is supposed to make life better for a family. It should liberate the parents by putting an end to an unhappy relationship and the accompanying fighting, stress, and anger. Most of the problems that crop up in the crisis years are of finite duration. They lessen as soon as the parents recover emotionally and return to their former level of good, capable parenting. The parents might still be distressed about the divorce, but they have come to terms with it enough to get back on an even keel, build a new and perhaps more satisfying life, and put their children's well-being first. The young people in these families have a good chance of having a happy, stable life.

Families who run into trouble in the long run are ones in which the divorce has only made the parents more bitter, furious, depressed, or hopeless. The emotional and economic crises don't resolve themselves; the antagonism between the divorced couple continues and in many cases, intensifies over the years.[6]

The "Overburdened Child"

The children trapped in families in which the conflict remains unresolved report feeling that their childhood was overshadowed by the divorce. Dr. Wallerstein calls this syndrome the "Overburdened Child."[7] These young people find that their temporary role of caregiver becomes permanent. They grow up putting their needs second to their parents' needs because they fear that they are the only ones keeping their parents going. The children must assume the burden of taking care of an ill, emotionally unstable, drug- or alcohol-dependent, depressed, or enraged parent. They become protector, confidant, adviser, housekeeper, but no one is there for them to lean on in turn.[8] Very young children, some as young as six years old, must take responsibility for bringing themselves up.

Teenagers find this scenario particularly troubling as it ties them to their parent and home just when, developmentally, they need to start separating. Often, these young people feel that they were asked to sacrifice their childhoods and experience long-term resentment over the fact.[9]

Linda, a participant in the Wallerstein study, was five when her parents split up. Her mother became so depressed that she paid little attention to her daughter. At six years old, Linda was getting herself up for school, making her own meals, and putting herself to bed. Now fifteen, she has spent the last ten years taking care of her mother. "I felt it was my responsibility to make sure Mom was okay," Linda recalled. "She was drinking a lot so I would go out with her or I would stay home with her instead of playing or going to school."[10]

Young People as Weapons

A particularly distressing side of the Overburdened Child Syndrome occurs when furious parents involve their offspring in their ongoing war with each other. These parents use their children as weapons against one another. "Tell your father he better be on time with his support check this month or I'm dragging him back to court," one mother yelled as her daughter left to spend the weekend with her father. "Tell your mother to dress you better next time you come here. Why am I sending so much money if she's just going to let you look like that?" another father demanded. Back and forth, back and forth, the children are lodged like missiles between parents.

When children aren't being used as weapons, they are sometimes enlisted as actual soldiers in the war. One parent will ask them to spy on the other and report back on his or her sexual, financial, or social activities.[11] For example, Katie's mother asked her to make notes about her father and his new girlfriend. "How much money does he spend on her?" she would ask. "What? And he won't even pay for your new school shoes!"

Distressed parents often expect their children to take sides. Jared's mother refused to speak to him when he returned home from a visit with his father because she believed that if Jared still loved his dad, he couldn't possibly love her. Jared knew his father drank and lied. But still, he was his father and Jared wanted to spend time with him. His mother, however, expected that Jared would cut him out of his life as she herself had done.

Some parents, in trying to explain to their children what went wrong with the marriage, burden them with private details of their life as a couple that their children are not emotionally ready to handle, for example, parent's sexual needs, abusive behavior, drug dependency, or infidelities.[12] Meredith's father spent her visits asking her to live with him. "After all," he said, "we both know your mother is a liar. I told you how all those 'PTA meetings' were really excuses to sleep with that guy from the swim club, right?"

The Price Overburdened Children Pay

Parents of overburdened children are so consumed by their bitterness and sorrow, they often can't see what

64

effect their demands are having on the children. Or perhaps they can see but their pain runs so deep, they just can't help themselves. Young people are severely stressed or anguished when a parent asks them to take sides, uses them to hurt the other parent, or is critical of the other parent. Children want—and need—to be allowed to love both parents. They feel guilty when asked to behave disloyally toward a loved one, and are wounded to hear criticism of him or her.

If the parents are unrelenting in their pressure, young people are presented with the difficult choice of either choosing one parent over the other or emotionally distancing themselves from both parents. It's a no-win situation; each choice costs the young person a parent.[13]

Who's in Charge Here?

When parents are so preoccupied with their ex-partner, they often can't cope with providing limits, discipline, and structure for their children. Curfews fall by the wayside, schoolwork goes undone. After all, if the parents can't control their own lives, how can they possibly keep control of anyone else's? Other parents, feeling guilty over the breakup, will indulge their children in ways they never have previously. They'll buy them expensive presents or relax rules.

Initially, young people might find the new freedom exhilarating. In the long run, however, they crave order and routines. They become frightened when they sense that no one is in charge. They know that means they are not protected from the world and from their own rash impulses.[14]

Teenagers are particularly vulnerable to being given

too much responsibility. Parents don't question that an infant needs total care. Teens, however, appear completely capable, and they often are, in the physical sense. They can make a sandwich, do their own laundry, or drive themselves to school. But parents often make the mistake of confusing teenagers' ability to cope physically with an ability to cope emotionally. Adolescents need as much emotional and behavioral guidance as a child at any other stage. As they begin their initial forays into the world at large, they need to know that home is a secure refuge.[15] Teens left on their own have no anchor, no safe, dependable place. They are at great risk for getting involved with drugs, alcohol, or sex.[16]

The Frightened Rebel

When teenagers are enmeshed in their parents' unresolved conflicts or are left to fend for themselves, it can have serious repercussions on their developing sense of self.

Teenagers' developmental job is to start separating themselves from their parents and finding out who they are as individuals. "Adolescents become sensitive to the complexities of more mature friendships and romantic relationships . . . Emotionally, adolescents struggle to adapt to . . . internal biological and external social changes, while at the same time trying to carve out their own niche apart from their parents," wrote Neil Kalter in *Growing Up with Divorce*.[17]

These changes usually show up as the well-known teenage rebellion. Teens start fighting with their parents in new ways as they struggle to establish their own separate identities. They want to wear their hair differently, wear clothes of their own choosing, express their own opinions, and push the limits of their independence. As teens move away from their parents, they become more dependent on their friends. Peer acceptance takes on more importance than parental approval.

Teens who are in happy, intact families or who are part of well-functioning divorced ones can make the break successfully because they know that no matter how difficult their behavior is, their parents will still love them and provide shelter from the world when it becomes too overwhelming.

Overburdened teens have a more difficult time making the transition from child to adult; they become "frightened rebels." Frightened rebels don't dare mutiny against their parents for three reasons. The first is that if they are so preoccupied with taking care of an incapable parent, they can't rebel. They are too afraid of the very real possibility that the parent may crumble altogether if he or she senses the children "turning" against them. "First your father abuses me; now you too?!" is the attitude an unstable mother might take. Linda, mentioned previously, knew the truth that without her care, her mother might become drunk and harm herself.[18]

The second reason these teens can't separate is that they don't have the secure sense of their parents' love that other teens have. When they are so uncertain of their parents' interest and protection, they don't dare do anything that might push their mother and father further away. How can you rebel against a father when you see him only occasionally and you're struggling for every minute of his attention? How can you risk arguing with your mother if you are afraid that your dissent will cause her to show even less interest in your life?[19]

The third reason frightened rebels refuse to rock the boat is that there is less for them to rebel against. In many divorced families, life is chaotic. Mom is working and doesn't get home until eight o'clock at night, or Dad has a date and leaves his son home alone. Often, there is no parental figure there to see if the young person has eaten dinner, done his homework, or kept his curfew. You can't break the rules if there aren't any.[20]

What happens to a teen who doesn't rebel, doesn't learn to separate himself from his parents, and is afraid to venture out into the world? He doesn't learn how to survive in a competitive world and, as a consequence, may find his dreams and aspirations thwarted.[21]

Who Succeeds?

This report may sound pretty bleak. But we all know kids from disrupted families who are happy and well-adjusted and go on to lead successful lives. We also know the kids who never seem to recover. What controls who will succeed where others stumble? There are no hard and fast rules because of one simple, yet incontrovertible, fact: everyone is different. One teen may not be able to handle stress where it hardly affects another. Even within a family, siblings will react differently. Vincent, thirteen years old, had been sad and solitary since the day his father left. His sister, Briana, eleven years old, was excited when her father came to visit but was just as content when he wasn't there. Same father, same mother, same divorce and yet two completely different reactions.

Although a young person's reaction to a divorce is

unpredictable, some factors are known to contribute to how he or she will fare. The child who has the best chance for a good postdivorce adjustment will have the following:

- Parents who cooperate and don't fight openly.[22]
- Parents who protect their children from—and don't involve them in—their struggles with each other.[23]
- Ongoing, conflict-free, positive contact with both parents, which provides the children with a sense of being valued.[24]
- Parents who can remain close to their children without becoming dependent on them.[25]
- Parents who provide consistent discipline.[26]
- A structured environment with a regular routine.[27]
- An ongoing, stable relationship with another adult such as grandparent, aunt, uncle, or teacher if parents cannot provide the items listed above.[28]
- Financial security.[29]

Age and Birth Order

Young people's age at the time of the divorce also has an influence on how they will adjust. Younger children appear to suffer more than older children at the time of the divorce, but, over the years, the younger children recover better than the older ones. That is because younger children are more protected, so they don't have to cope with a lot of the turmoil that teens do. Another factor is that preschool families tend to restabilize faster because the mothers are younger and, therefore, more likely to remarry.[30]

Birth order is also a factor as parents will naturally

expect more from the oldest child than from the younger ones. The oldest usually ends up taking the brunt of the divorce by assuming more responsibilities and becoming more enmeshed in the parents' conflict.

Is the Glass Half-Empty or Half-Full?

Does divorce have long-term effects on young people? Which of the various experts are right: those that say young people continue to suffer years after the fact or those that say time heals the pain? Perhaps both sides are right; maybe it just depends on how you choose to look at it. Frank Furstenberg, in his book *Divided Families*, discussed a study in which it was found that 34 percent of young people from disrupted families had discipline problems at school while only 20 percent of young people from intact families did. These figures can be looked at two different ways, he said. You can point to the finding that the children of divorce had more problems than the children from intact families or you can focus on the fact that 66 percent of children from divorced families did not have behavioral problems.[31]

As Furstenberg wrote, "The glass is half-empty or half-full, depending on one's point of view."[32]

7

Living in Stepfamilies

Sixteen-year-old Duncan slammed the back door as he stomped out of the house. His mother and her boyfriend, Fred, had just told him that they were getting married. "You just left Dad! Now you're already moving in with someone else? What kind of mother are you?" he had yelled. Duncan was still deeply hurt over his parents' sudden divorce a year ago; now he was expected to deal with being part of a new family, a family to which he felt no connection. He thought Fred was a whiny jerk, and he hated Fred's "snotty" little daughter. But most of all, Duncan was furious that major decisions were being made that intimately affected him and he had no say in the matter. "I can't wait until I'm eighteen and I can get out of this nuthouse for good!" Duncan thought angrily as he gunned his car out of the driveway.

If your parents have divorced, there's a good chance

that you are going to become part of a stepfamily. Four out of five divorced people remarry within five years.[1] The National Survey of Children projected that approximately one fourth of all young people will live with at least one stepparent at some point.[2] Back in 1982, it was estimated that almost fifteen million young people lived with remarried parents.[3] If you include young people who live with one biological parent but visit a noncustodial parent and stepparent, the number of kids who have contact with stepfamily living rises dramatically.[4]

Stepfamilies: They Take Work

Although a parent's remarriage can provide many positive things to a young person—both emotional and financial security, and good role models—living in a stepfamily is not easy. It takes a lot of dedication and flexibility on everyone's part to achieve a comfortable life.

The prevailing myth about stepfamilies is that when parents remarry, the new family unit becomes just like a "normal" family. But there is really nothing "normal" about it. People who barely know each other are thrown together and are expected to share intimate living quarters and to love each other instantaneously. And when parents remarry, the children acquire not just a new stepparent, but a complex and confusing family tree. Suddenly, there can be four parents, eight sets of grandparents, stepsiblings, half siblings, aunts, uncles, cousins, stepaunts, stepuncles, and stepcousins. And if any of these new relatives have divorced and remarried, you can see how relationships can spiral beyond comprehension. To further complicate matters, the children of the families

72

are often still mourning the loss of their previous family unit when presented with this dizzying crowd.

The truth is that biological families have years to get to know each other and develop a living style. Stepfamilies are given about as much time as it takes to walk down the aisle. Most young people, expecting some sort of *Brady Bunch* harmony, are surprised by the amount of work it takes to achieve it. Teens, in particular, feel angry. They are seeking independence, but are expected to stick close to home to get to know their new family better.[5]

All stepfamily members have to realize that life rarely imitates television. Jan Brady never left for court-ordered weekend visits with her father. Greg Brady never struggled with sexual feelings for his three attractive stepsisters. Marcia was never in a rage because Mr. Brady, her stepfather, dared to ground her. These kinds of situations happen in real life. The stresses and dynamics must be acknowledged and dealt with if a stepfamily is to succeed.

Letting Go and Moving Forward

Young people may feel angry and betrayed by a parent's impending remarriage because it means they have to let go of their fantasy that their biological parents will reunite.[6] When they see their parent say "I do" to someone else, they have to accept the divorce once and for all. They can no longer fool themselves that life may someday go back to the way they once knew it. And by accepting that, they are forced to face an uncertain future with another adult, whom they don't know well enough yet to trust. Some young people, refusing to deal with this truth, may go so far as to try to sabotage their parent's new marriage in the hope that the two parents can still get back together.[7]

"If You're His Wife, Are You Still My Mother?"

When parents remarry, young people are often initially fearful. Young people can be frightened that they will be replaced in their parent's heart by this new relationship. This is especially true if the biological parent has been single for a long time and has forged a special bond with his or her child, a sort of "It's us against the world" mentality.[8] Fifteen-year-old Randall, whose parents split when he was two, was upset when his mother suddenly remarried. "What does she need him for? We've always been okay on our own!" he said.

Young people don't always understand that the love between a man and a woman is very different from the love between a parent and a child. The former can change; the latter is forever. But young people, confusing the two, have already seen from the divorce that love can end. They fear that once a parent remarries, the parent's love for them may be transferred to the new partner.

Sometimes this fear shows itself as jealousy. Young people may become jealous of a stepparent's relationship with a parent because it is depriving them of the undivided attention they used to have, erroneously confirming their fear that their parent loves them less than previously. This may result in a competition between the child and the stepparent. Who can get the most attention from the parent, thus proving that he or she is loved the most?[9]

"My Parents Don't Do THAT!"

Another issue young people have to confront in stepfamilies is a loaded one: their parents' sexuality. Many young people find the idea that their parents have sex for pleasure rather than just to have children deeply disturbing. They find it difficult enough to deal with their own sexual feelings—the thought that their parents are having these same urges is a very tough one to handle. When a child lives in an intact family, it is easy to dismiss the idea. As fourteen-year-old Stacy said, "My parents are so out of it, they probably haven't done it in years." But if, after the divorce, Mom starts wearing seductive dresses for dates or there is a strange woman in Dad's bed, that theory goes out the window.[10]

Teens, whose own sexual impulses are developing full force, have a particularly hard time with this subject. It's embarrassing and uncomfortable. If a parent remarries or has a partner move in with them, the teen then has no escape from the tension. As teens get older and learn to accept their own sexual feelings, however, they find it easier to accept their parents' needs.[11]

The Early Years of a Stepfamily

The myth that a stepparent and child will immediately love one another just because the parent loves both of them is a big hurdle to overcome in the beginning of a stepfamily. A young person may think the stepparent is okay, the stepparent may think the child is likable, but in reality, they haven't had time enough together to say they truly love each other. Young people may also be afraid to allow themselves to love, or even like, stepparents for fear that these marriages will bust up just the way their parents' did.[12] Many stepparents and stepchildren feel guilty about their mixed feelings, but love is something that grows over time; it can't be ordered or forced.

It may come as no surprise that the younger the children are, the easier it is to achieve a harmonious stepfamily life.[13] Younger children don't have as much of a memory of the original family so they can accept more easily a stepparent as a substitute parent. Teens, however, have a harder time adjusting because they have a strong attachment to the original family unit. They also have more problems accepting a new and additional authority figure at a time in their lives when any authority is becoming suspect. Just when they are trying to establish independence, here come some more people who think they can tell them what to do![14]

Many stepfamilies are unprepared for these confusing emotions and consequently find the first few years together very rocky as members fight for control, independence, and attention while trying to establish roles. A stepparent may assume the role of parent too quickly—acting the disciplinarian and setting rules.[15] The young person may rebel, thinking, "You're not my real father. Who are you to tell me what to do!" Or the stepparent, feeling uncomfortable about asserting authority, may step back and not deal with the children at all. Some young people may fear that this means the stepparent doesn't like them. Other stepparents are uncertain about their position in the family: "Am I a parent or a friend to my stepchildren?" They may act inconsistently as a result. Seth's stepfather would order him to clean his room one day, and the next, sit in the backyard and set off firecrackers with him.[16]

Guilty, Guilty, Guilty

The question of loyalty becomes a big dilemma for young people with stepparents.[17] They feel guilty if they like their new stepparent because that makes them feel disloyal to their biological parent, especially if that parent is still angry or depressed over the divorce. "How can I like Dad's wife when she makes Mom so unhappy? Will Mom stop loving me if I think Jenny is fun?" asked thirteen-year-old Faye. This tension is magnified if stepparents ask that the stepchildren call them "Dad" or "Mom" before the stepchildren feel ready to do so.[18] Young people often fight this precarious situation by pulling back from, or acting angrily with, the stepparents.[19]

Stepsisters, Stepbrothers

When parents remarry, stepparents aren't the only new factor in the family equation. Very often, stepparents come with their own children. The two sets of kids, even if they live in separate houses, have to get to know and adjust to each other as well. Again, it takes a while for everyone to figure out their place in this new family. The young person who used to be the oldest in his family may now find himself displaced by older stepsiblings. He is shocked to discover he is no longer king of the mountain. A youngest child, reveling in all the perks that go with being the baby, may be upset to find a younger stepchild grabbing all that attention.[20]

Stepsiblings may also have to give up their uniqueness in terms of gender.[21] Gayle always felt special because she was the only daughter. But when her mother remarried, suddenly she was sharing her room with two stepsisters. She felt she had become just one of a crowd of girls.

The stepsiblings may become rivals for their parents' attention. Biological children can feel intensely jealous when their parent shows concern for their stepsibling. "Who is this kid taking Mom's time away from me?!" they think. They panic because they are afraid there won't be enough love to go around.[22]

If the young people can adjust to this new setup and learn to share space, parents, and attention, many find that they really enjoy having stepsiblings. They become good friends and allies, who understand each other's difficulties in living with divorce and their parents' sometimes unfathomable behavior.

A New Baby in the House

Young people have some more adjusting to do if the remarried couple has a new baby. The older half siblings can feel pushed out or replaced.[23] As Clem, age fourteen, said, "Kenny, my baby brother, is related to both my Dad and my stepmom. It makes me think, 'What do they need me for?' They've got a new and better family. I'm just this kid who shows up every other week. Where do I fit in?"

Blending Two Families

Many experts have taken to replacing the word stepfamily, with its negative connotations of wicked stepmothers and neglected stepchildren, with the more positive term blended family. It's a good choice because one of the biggest jobs stepfamilies have to undertake is the blending of two separate families' cultures, traditions, and routines.

Every family does things differently, and when two are thrown together, they must negotiate how this new household will run. While they are working this out, very unimportant issues can become magnified until they seem insurmountable: "But we always had turkey on Thanksgiving!" "But we always had ham!" Or, "We never ate dinner in front of the TV!" "We loved watching a movie while we ate!" Or, "The kitchen towel goes over the cabinet door!" "No, it doesn't! It goes through the refrigerator door handle."

Young people can get very upset about these discussions even though they sound so silly on paper. They are so unsure about their future in this new family, they need to depend on what little stability they know: that Christmas presents will be opened Christmas Eve, not in the morning; that the ketchup will be kept in the refrigerator, not in the pantry; that Friday night will still be family video night.[24]

Stepfamilies do a delicate dance as they decide which routines to keep, which ones no longer work, and where to create new ones altogether.[25] Each member has to decide where and how much he or she is willing to compromise in order to make this new family work.

If It's Tuesday, This Must Be Dad's House . . .

Many young people aren't part of just one stepfamily, but two: their biological mother's and their biological father's. Shuttling between the two households can be confusing and unsettling. They are expected to remember two sometimes contradictory sets of household rules and behave accordingly.[26] For example, at Lillian's mother's house, she is allowed to stay out until ten o'clock on weeknights as long as her homework gets done first. At her father's house, however, she is not allowed out at all on school nights. At her mother's house, dinner is a loud, noisy affair where everyone shares the events of the day. But at her father's house, "My stepmom always has a headache or something so we're not supposed to even breathe during dinner," Lillian reported. "I feel like I'm getting a split personality."

Some young people feel tentative about where they fit in, not feeling wholly a part of either family. They can feel especially awkward when visiting their noncustodial parent. They aren't truly a member of that household because they don't live there; yet they are something more than just a visitor.[27]

This ambiguity poses a dilemma for parents and their spouses. Should the visiting children be expected to do chores like the live-in kids? Or should they be entertained since they are only there for a short while?[28] Young people pick up on the parents' uncertainty. Some use it to play one parent off against the other in order to get their own way. "Mom never makes us do our own laundry!" Or, "Dad thinks I'm old enough to drive!" Some parents, already torn with guilt over what the divorce has done to the children, find it difficult to be cast as the "mean" parent and give in, which confuses the children even more.[29] It is frightening to them to feel that they, and not their parents, are in charge.

Teens can be especially confused by having two families. In the process of separating from home, they evaluate their parents' beliefs to see which they will keep as an adult. Children involved in two stepfamilies, however, have to sort through two sets of values and attitudes, both of which are being presented to them as the best way to live.[30]

The Positive Side of Stepfamily Living

This chapter might make you think that there is nothing good to be gained from living in a stepfamily. Not so. Just because a stepfamily situation can be difficult and challenging, it doesn't mean it isn't worth fighting out. If all members of a stepfamily really make an effort to work out the kinks, the children can win many wonderful rewards.

- If a young person's relationship with a biological parent is rocky or nonexistent, the same-sex stepparent can provide a good role model, love, and support that the young person might not have otherwise.

- If a young person is made to feel very much a key part of the new stepfamily—if the parent and stepparent make the child feel included—it can raise the young person's self-esteem.[31]

- If the parent and stepparent have a close, caring relationship, they show their stepchildren that marriages don't have to be filled with anger, fighting, and betrayal. The children have a healthy role model of a mutually supportive couple.[32]

- Remarriage can end the financial stresses of living in a single family home,[33] which were discussed in Chapter 3.

- Living in a stepfamily teaches a young person how to compromise and adapt, skills that are much needed for getting along in the outside world.[34]
- Stepbrothers and stepsisters can provide each other with friendship and support they might not have gotten in their own immediate, nuclear family.[35]
- Stepfamilies ask that the young people grow up faster than they would have normally. This makes it easier for them to leave home and live on their own when the time comes to do so.[36]

Happy Endings

Kerry's mother married Pat when Kerry was ten years old. Kerry resented him from the start. "He was always in my business," she remembers now. "Asking me questions, telling me what to do. I probably said at least a hundred times, 'You're not my REAL father. You can't order me around!' I knew that really hurt him because he really wanted to be a part of my life."

Despite their fights, however, when Kerry was to be married, she wanted both her father and Pat to walk her down the aisle. "Dad's great. He gave me life. But Pat's the one who raised me and stood by me even when I was horrible to him. When I got busted for drugs, he was the one who came to the police station and got me. I never thought I'd say this, but I love Pat. He's really been there for me. I know now that I need both Dad *and* Pat in my life."

8

The Future

Twenty-year-old Camille ran a hand worriedly through her blond curls. Her boyfriend, Daniel, was a half-hour late picking her up for their date. Although one part of her knew that he was probably just held up in traffic, another part, a part she could not control, felt a wild panic. Her thoughts began to race: "He's late because he is with another woman. I know it. I know he's cheating on me. How could I have been so stupid to trust him!" She began to flash back on all the times her mother paced the floor, waiting for her father to come home, and on all the times, after her parents' divorce, Camille hung out by the front door, waiting in vain for her dad to visit her. She had that same suffocating feeling now.

When Daniel finally showed up, covered in grease from fixing a flat tire, Camille had already made up her mind to break up with him. "I just can't trust him," she thought. "He may have had a good excuse this time, but really, men are just bound to let you down eventually. Better to get out now, before he can hurt me."

What happens when children of divorce become adults? Are their parents' mistakes destined to haunt them forever? Or can they break away from their families' histories and create new, better lives for themselves?

The answer is not that clear-cut. Many children of divorce can—and do—go on to make more fulfilling, stable lives for themselves. Some even find that there are positive effects of their parents' divorce. Since they had to grow up faster than their peers, they became more independent, competent, and resourceful at an earlier age.[1] This makes their adjustment to leaving home for college or their first job easier.

The other side of the coin, however, is that many children of divorce do have a difficult time making a successful transition to adulthood. According to Silvio Silvestri, Ph.D., of the Center for Adult Children of Divorce, South Lake Tahoe, California, children of divorce are four times more likely to divorce than young people from intact families.[2]

Why are some affected while others are not? What makes the difference?

Who Breaks Free?

Although divorce will always be stressful to young people, it is not true that all are fated to a lifetime of unhappiness. Many overcome the emotional upheaval and go on to have contented lives. There are a variety of factors that make the difference in how a child of divorce makes the leap to adulthood. They are listed in Chapter 6, but here is an abbreviated version:

- How the divorce was handled in the family. Were the children protected or did they witness fighting and anger?[3]
- What went on in the postdivorce family. Were the parents able to rebuild new lives that were better than the one lived by the intact family?[4]
- The inner resources of the children to differentiate themselves from their parents. Do they have enough self-confidence and strength to say, "Those were my parents' lives, not ours—we can have something better?"[5]
- If the parents were emotionally unavailable, was there another adult—a grandparent, teacher, friend—who provided a good role model?[6]

Many experts feel that these factors are even more important in predicting future success or failure than how young people react at the time of the divorce. If young people get angry, sad, withdrawn, or fearful when their parents split up, the above factors will play a key part in whether they will be able to work those feelings out or be forever held back by them. Camille, for example, was very distraught when her parents' marriage fell apart when she was eight. But if, from that time forward, her father had been dependable, or her mother had overcome her bitterness and anger, maybe Camille would not now be so fearful of betrayal by men.[7]

Taking a Chance on Love

Love relationships all involve risk. There is always the chance that the other person will hurt you or you will

hurt him or her. Young adults from happy, intact families are willing to take that chance because they have seen
that a good relationship can provide love, support,
companionship, and security. Children of divorce, however, only see that marriage is a source of unhappiness
and instability—especially if their parents divorced more
than once. Because of that, many young adults from disrupted families run into emotional trouble when they
start looking for their own love relationships. They know
how deeply a failed relationship hurts, so they react in
two ways: either they become afraid to take a chance on
love at all,[8] or they try to take complete control of the
situation.[9]

"When these kids were growing up, they had no
control over their lives," explained Dr. Howard Yekell,
psychologist and clinical supervisor of the Open Center,
Shrewsbury, New Jersey. "Now they want to control
everything, but you can't control another person." This
need for control has a couple of effects. The young
adults may marry too early, hoping to establish stability
and a hold over their partners. Or they may wait an unreasonable amount of time to marry, looking for some
sign from the heavens that their partners will remain
committed for life. They are terrified of betrayal and,
like Camille, are constantly on the alert for any sign of
it.[10]

Many young adults also fear that they will be the
ones to betray their partners. They assume that they are
destined to be like their mothers or fathers.[11] Aaron, seventeen, was afraid that he would never find the love he
craved because, over the last few years, he had dated several girls and broken up with all of them. "I'm just like

my father," he said, with a tremble in his voice that was at odds with his usually cocky demeanor. "He's already on wife number four and she's not that much older than me! I don't want a life like that, but I can see I'm already going that way. I just can't stick it out with one girl." Aaron didn't understand that most teens date briefly and then move on. They figure out what they want—and don't want—in a relationship by having various dating experiences. It doesn't mean they will always be so un-committed. But Aaron saw his perfectly appropriate search as a character flaw in himself.

Delayed Reaction

In addition to all the above concerns, researchers are finding that girls sometimes have additional problems to work out when they come of age. There is a syndrome that Dr. Judith Wallerstein called the "Sleeper Effect"[12] and Dr. Neil Kalter named the "Timebomb Effect."[13] In essence, they both described the same thing: young women, who seemed to have adjusted well to their par-ents' break–up and showed no signs of emotional distress, fall apart when they become old enough to have serious romantic relationships. This seems to happen much more often to girls because girls seem to fare much better psychologically immediately after divorce than boys.[14]

These young women think they will never find real love; some don't believe it even exists except in the mov-ies. They fear loss and betrayal to an unreasonable degree, and this wreaks major havoc in their emotional lives.[15]

Camille, as we have seen, coped by rejecting her

boyfriend before he could get the chance to reject her. Amanda, twenty-four years old, kept a string of four or five boyfriends on the line at any given moment. "If one of them bugs off, I've always got another. None of them can hurt me," she said. Melinda solved her dilemma by marrying a much-older man when she was only nineteen. She freely admitted that Carl was not the love of her life but he made her feel secure because she knew he'd be less likely to abandon her than a "wild" young boy her age. Lauren married the first boy who asked her because she thought he was her only chance to get out of her house and establish some stability. She was divorced within two years. Maureen avoided the issue altogether by throwing herself into her career as a lawyer and refusing to date.

None of these choices have worked because none of these women are happy. They have worked so hard at keeping their anxieties at bay that now they have no idea what they really want from life. As Maureen admitted, "I'm just treading water, doing everything I can to keep from going under. I don't dare ask for anything more than that."

Lonely Boys, Aimless Lives

Young men from disrupted homes don't get hit with the Sleeper/Timebomb Effect as much as young women do, but this is not to say that they don't carry their own special burdens as they approach adulthood.

Since the majority of boys are in their mothers' custody, they grow up without a same-sex role model in the house. They don't see Dad get up every morning and go to work. They don't see how he handles pressure, responsibility, and emotions on a day-to-day basis. So when it comes time for them to leave home and act like mature, adult males, they aren't really sure what that means. "Boys don't just grow up with a solid sense of their own masculinity; they have to find someone to emulate. But even fathers who are involved with their sons after the divorce might be seeing them only every other week. That's not enough contact," explained Dr. Kalter.[16]

It's as if boys with solid male role models are given a map of how to live their lives. Boys without role models don't have that map so they don't know where they are going. The result? Many of these young men find it difficult to commit to careers and relationships. They appear aimless, dabbling in dead-end jobs or inappropriate romances. In Dr. Wallerstein's study, ten years after their parents' divorce, almost one half of the young men were unhappy, lonely, and unsuccessful with love relationships.[17] More than a third of the nineteen-to twenty-three-year-olds had no set goals, a limited education, and a sense that their lives were out of their control.[18]

"Something was missing in these young men's transitions from children to adults. It takes time—sometimes into their thirties—for them to struggle through this, to figure out how to get what they want instead of just being bitter about what they didn't have," said Howard Yekell.[19]

Breaking the Cycle

Young people can break the cycle of unhappiness. First, they must realize that they are not their parents. They are in control of their own lives, and they are not doomed or destined to relive their families' pain.

The primary task for these young people is to realize why they are feeling the way they do. That may sound simplistic, but many young people can't make the connection between how they feel at twenty and a divorce that may have happened fifteen years before. If young people can make that realization—that their emotions are connected to old wounds—sometimes they are able to resolve their own conflicts. They need to separate past and present, and say to themselves, "My parents are my parents and I am me. I have my own life, and I don't have to repeat what happened to them. I can create my own destiny."[20]

For example, Cady, nineteen, became depressed when she left for college. "When I first went away, I felt overwhelmed, cut off. I just cried constantly. I didn't know why," she reported. "Then I really dug into myself and I realized I had been feeling homeless for a number of years. I had been kicked between my Mom and Dad for such a long time that going away made me afraid I had lost what little hold I had on them. Like 'Well, she's all grown up now. We don't have to deal with her anymore.' I talked to them about it, and they assured me that they might not be the best parents but they were *my* parents for life!"

Young people can also help each other. They can organize groups with other young people from similar backgrounds to discuss how they are feeling and how they cope. "Teens often feel alone with their thoughts and emotions about how their parents got along and how that might continue to affect them. It is frustrating and lonely to not have any place to take those thoughts. They really need to get a handle on them and a discussion group with their peers is an excellent spot," said Dr. Kalter.[21]

If teens are having trouble pulling together such a group, parents should lobby the school board, the local community center, or a church or synagogue to set one up. "The traditional family isn't so commonplace anymore so there will be a lot of kids who would sign up for such a group or course," said Howard Yekell.[22]

Adults other than parents can also provide help. If young people are struggling to find role models who offer a more stable vision of life than their parents, they can seek out grandparents, aunts, uncles, teachers, coaches, or neighbors who are willing to spend time with them and show them a better way of life. If a parent remarries happily, a stepparent can demonstrate by example that marriage can be warm and loving.[23]

Young people who find that these coping methods are inadequate should seek psychological therapy. "With help, they can become aware of what the old potential conflicts are and what they might have absorbed just by being around parents who didn't get along," said Dr. Kalter.[24] If money is a problem, young people can ask their family doctors or guidance counselors if they know any clinics in the area that provide such a service free or at a reduced cost.

Moving On

If you are a child of divorce, your life changed dramatically when your family split up. That may have been frightening, but as you get older you realize that life is a series of changes and transitions. With each new step in life, you become a little bit different, more independent, more capable, and a lot wiser. And that new, ever-evolving person doesn't have to march down the same road his or her parents did. You can chart your own path, one that no one in your family has ever followed. You don't have to follow anyone's map but your own. It's time now to learn what you can from the past and move on.

Helpful Organizations

Alateen. If your parents are breaking up because one or both have a problem with alcohol, Alateen can help. Call your local Alcoholics Anonymous group to find out about Alateen.

American Association for Marriage and Family Therapy. 1100 17th Street NW, Washington, D.C. 20036. Referral line: 1-800-374-2638. This group can provide referrals to therapists in any area of the country.

Banana Splits. Interact Publishers. 1-800-359-0961. These peer support groups for children of divorce are organized in schools under the supervision of a counselor or teacher.

National Child Abuse Hotline. 1-800-4-A-CHILD. Call this number if you are being physically, mentally, or sexually abused. This is a twenty-four-hour national child abuse hotline that provides intervention, information, and referrals to local support groups.

Divorce Anonymous. 2600 Colorado Avenue, Suite 270, Santa Monica, CA 90404. 310-998-6538. These groups are located in eight midwest and western states. They provide emotional support and information to divorcing families.

Al-Anon Family Group. 1372 Broadway, 7th Floor, New York, NY 10019. 1-800-356-9996. This is a nonprofit organization with a network of agencies that counsel families.

Gamateen. If your parents are divorcing because one or both are gamblers, call your local Gamblers Anonymous to find out about Gamateen.

Legal Aid Society. If you are having legal problems or are unsure of your rights, call your local Legal Aid Society. If they can't help you, they can refer you to someone who can.

Rainbows. 708-310-1880. These peer support groups are for children of divorce or children who have had a parent die and are organized through local churches or schools.

Stepfamily Association of America. 1-800-735-0329. This organization can find you a "step" support group, an appropriate therapist, and provide you with information about stepfamily living.

Check also with your local church, synagogue, school board, and community center. They often run support groups or workshops for young people whose parents are divorced.

Chapter Notes

Chapter 1

1. Beth Levine, "Children of Divorce," *Seventeen* (January 1990), pp. 95, 110, 111.

2. Ibid.

3. Frank F. Furstenberg, Jr., and Andrew J. Cherlin, *Divided Families: What Happens to Children When Parents Part* (Cambridge, Mass.: Harvard University Press, 1991), p. 11.

4. Ibid.

5. Neil Kalter, *Growing Up with Divorce: Helping Your Child Avoid Immediate and Later Emotional Problems* (New York: The Free Press, 1990), p. 1.

6. Furstenberg, and Cherlin, p. 14.

7. Judith S. Wallerstein and Sandra Blakeslee, *Second Chances: Men, Women and Children a Decade After Divorce* (New York: Ticknor & Fields, 1990), p. 298.

Chapter 2

1. Arlene Richards and Irene Willis, *How to Get It Together When Your Parents Are Coming Apart* (New York: David McKay Company, 1976), pp. 1–43.

2. Robert E. Emery, *Marriage, Divorce and Children's Adjustment* (Newbury Park, Calif.: Sage Publications, 1988), p. 94.

3. Frank F. Furstenberg, Jr., and Andrew J. Cherlin, *Divided Families: What Happens to Children When Parents Part* (Cambridge, Mass.: Harvard University Press, 1991), p. 19.

4. Ibid. p. 21.

5. Richards and Willis, p. 49.

6. Ibid. p. 19.

7. Furstenberg and Cherlin, p. 64.

8. Richards and Willis, p. 46.

9. Howard Pobiner, divorce lawyer, White Plains, N.Y., personal interview, April 1993.

10. Eda LeShan, *What's Going to Happen to Me?* (New York: Four Winds Press, 1978), p. 14.

11. Richards and Willis, p. 5.

12. LeShan, pp. 4, 28.

13. Ibid. p. 18.

Chapter 3

1. Howard Pobiner, divorce lawyer, White Plains, N.Y., personal interview, April 1993.

2. Ibid.

3. Frank F. Furstenberg, Jr., and Andrew J. Cherlin, *Divided Families: What Happens to Children When Parents Part* (Cambridge, Mass.: Harvard University Press, 1991), p. 32.

4. Ibid.

5. Robert E. Emery, *Marriage, Divorce and Children's Adjustment* (Newbury Park, Calif.: Sage Publications, 1988), p. 128.

6. *The Friend of the Court Handbook*, Oakland County, Mich.

7. Pobiner, personal interview, April 1993.

8. Stanley S. Clawar, "One House, Two Cars, Three Kids," *Family Advocate* (Fall 1982), pp. 15–17.

9. Pobiner, personal interview, April 1993.

10. Emery, p. 132.

11. Pobiner, personal interview, April 1993.

12. Ibid.

13. Arlene Richards and Irene Willis, *How to Get It Together When Your Parents Are Coming Apart* (New York: David McKay Company, 1976), p. 61.

14. Pobiner, personal interview, April 1993.

15. Furstenberg and Cherlin, p. 23.

16. Ibid. p. 65.

17. Emery, p. 108.

18. Cherlin p. 27.

19. Judith S. Wallerstein, Ph.D., founder and executive director of the Center for the Family in Transition, Corte Madera, Calif., personal interview, December 1988.

20. Richards and Willis, p. 69.

21. Eda LeShan, *What's Going to Happen to Me?* (New York: Four Winds Press, 1978), p. 69.

22. Richards and Willis, p. 77.

Chapter 4

1. Maxine Rock, "Is Divorce Really the Answer?," *Woman's Day* (September 21, 1993), pp. 52–53, 132, 134.

2. Judith S. Wallerstein, Ph.D., founder and executive director of the Center for the Family in Transition, Corte Madera, Calif., personal interview, June 1989.

3. Robert E. Emery, *Marriage, Divorce and Children's Adjustment* (Newbury Park, Calif.: Sage Publications, 1988), p. 100.

4. Leslie Morgan, "The Case of the Missing Father," *Seventeen* (January 1991), pp. 92–93.

5. Pamela Redmond Satran, "How to Say No to Divorce," *Family Circle* (February 1, 1990), pp. 31–32.

6. Frank F. Furstenberg, Jr., and Andrew J. Cherlin, *Divided Families: What Happens to Children When Parents Part* (Cambridge, Mass.: Harvard University Press, 1991), p. 53.

7. Morgan, pp. 92–93.

8. Rock, pp. 52–53, 132, 134.

9. Satran, pp. 31–32.

10. Furstenberg and Cherlin, p. 50.

11. Emery, p. 13.

12. Furstenberg and Cherlin, p. 55.

13. Ibid.

14. Ibid. p. 54.

15. Wallerstein, personal interview, June 1989.

16. Neil Kalter, *Growing Up with Divorce: Helping Your Child Avoid Immediate and Later Emotional Problems* (New York: The Free Press, 1990), p. 22.

17. Ibid.

18. Judith S. Wallerstein and Sandra Blakeslee, *Second Chances: Men, Women and Children a Decade After Divorce* (New York: Ticknor & Fields, 1990), p. 156.

Chapter 5

1. Robert E. Emery, *Marriage, Divorce and Children's Adjustment* (Newbury Park, Calif.: Sage Publications, 1988), p. 87.

2. Ibid.

3. Silvio Silvestri, Ph.D., director of the Center for Adult Children of Divorce, South Lake Tahoe, Calif., personal interview, June 1993.

4. Frank F. Furstenberg, Jr., and Andrew J. Cherlin, *Divided Families: What Happens to Children When*

Parents Part (Cambridge, Mass.: Harvard University Press, 1991), p. 37.

5. Emery, p. 88.

6. Furstenberg and Cherlin, p. 36.

7. Howard Pobiner, divorce lawyer, White Plains, N.Y., personal interview, April 1993.

8. Judith S. Wallerstein and Sandra Blakeslee, *Second Chances: Men, Women and Children a Decade After Divorce* (New York: Ticknor & Fields, 1990), p. 136.

9. Ibid.

10. U.S. Census Bureau, personal interview, June 1993.

11. Furstenberg and Cherlin, p. 39.

12. Ibid. p. 40.

13. Ibid. p. 38.

14. Ibid. p. 37.

15. Ibid. p. 38.

16. Wallerstein and Blakeslee, p. 144.

17. Furstenberg, p. 38.

18. Ibid. p. 60.

19. Wallerstein and Blakeslee, p. 150.

20. Eda LeShan, *What's Going to Happen to Me?* (New York: Four Winds Press, 1978), p. 74.

21. Judith S. Wallerstein, Ph.D., founder and executive director of the Center for the Family in Transition, Corte Madera, Calif., personal interview, June 1989.

22. Neil Kalter, *Growing Up with Divorce: Helping Your Child Avoid Immediate and Later Emotional Problems* (New York: The Free Press, 1990), p. 323.

23. Wallerstein, personal interview, June 1989.

24. Kalter, p. 340.

Chapter 6

1. Beth Levine, "Children of Divorce," *Seventeen* (January 1990), pp. 95, 110, 111.

2. Frank F. Furstenberg, Jr., and Andrew J. Cherlin, *Divided Families: What Happens to Children When Parents Part* (Cambridge Mass.: Harvard University Press, 1991), p. 65.

3. Ibid. p. 66.

4. Judith S. Wallerstein and Sandra Blakeslee, *Second Chances: Men, Women and Children a Decade After Divorce* (New York: Ticknor & Fields, 1990), p. 186.

5. Anthony Brandt, "Children of Divorce: From Hurt to Healing," *Parenting* (October 1991), pp. 119, 121, 123, 125.

6. Wallerstein and Blakeslee, p. 135.

7. Ibid. p. 184.

8. Ibid. p. 184.

9. Neil Kalter, *Growing Up with Divorce: Helping Your Child Avoid Immediate and Later Emotional Problems* (New York: The Free Press, 1990), p. 15.

10. Wallerstein, pp. 198–200.

11. Ibid. p. 189.

12. Kalter, p. 13.

13. Robert E. Emery, *Marriage Divorce and Children's Adjustment* (Newbury Park, Calif.: Sage Publications, 1988), pp. 110–111.

14. Eda LeShan, *What's Going to Happen to Me?* (New York: Four Winds Press, 1978), pp. 71–72.

15. Wallerstein and Blakeslee, pp. 167–169.

16. Kalter, p. 310.

17. Ibid. p. 309.

18. Judith S. Wallerstein, Ph.D., founder and executive director of the Center for the family in Transition, Corte Madera, Calif., personal interview, June 1989.

19. Ibid.

20. Ibid.

21. Wallerstein and Blakeslee, p. 151.

22. Furstenberg and Cherlin, p. 71.

23. Wallerstein and Blakeslee, p. 180.

24. Ibid.

25. Ibid. p. 187.

26. Emery, p. 109.

27. Wallerstein and Blakeslee, p. 181.

28. Wallerstein, personal interview, June 1989.

29. Furstenberg and Cherlin, p. 71.

30. Wallerstein, person interview, June 1989.

31 Furstenberg and Cherlin, p. 69.

32. Ibid.

Chapter 7

1. Elizabeth Einstein, *The Stepfamily: Living, Loving & Learning* (Boston, Mass.: Shambhala, 1985), p. 20.

2. Frank F. Furstenberg, Jr., and Andrew J. Cherlin, *Divided Families: What Happens to Children When Parents Part* (Cambridge, Mass.: Harvard University Press, 1991), p. 14.

3. Einstein, p. 5.

4. Furstenberg and Cherlin, p. 14.

5. Einstein, p. 173.

6. Neil Kalter, *Growing Up with Divorce: Helping Your Child Avoid Immediate and Later Emotional Problems* (New York: The Free Press, 1990), p. 21.

7. Linda Bird Francke, *Growing Up Divorced: Helping Your Child* (New York: Linden Press/Simon & Schuster, 1983), p. 188.

8. Einstein, p. 20.

9. Kalter, p. 21.

10. Francke, p. 171.

11. Ibid. p. 175.

12. Ibid. p. 188–198.

13. Robert E. Emery, *Marriage, Divorce and Children's Adjustment* (Newbury Park, Calif.: Sage Publications, 1988), p. 98.

14. Einstein, p. 132.

15. Kalter, p. 337.

16. Francke, pp. 188–198.

17. Kalter, p. 19.

18. Einstein, p. 60.

19. Ibid. pp. 12–13.

20. Ibid. p. 72.

21. Mary Ann Artlip, James A. Artlip, and Earl S. Saltzman, *The New American Family: Tools for Strengthening Step-Families* (Lancaster, Pa.: Starburst Publishers, 1993), p. 118.

22. Francke, p. 117.

23. Ibid. pp. 204–205.

24. Artlip, pp. 163–164.

25. Furstenberg, pp. 83–84.

26. Artlip, p. 161.

27. Einstein, p. 13.

28. Artlip, p. 155.

29. Einstein, p. 95.

30. Ibid. p. 173.

31. Judith S. Wallerstein, Ph.D., founder and executive director of the Center for the Family in Transition, Corte Madera, Calif., personal interview, June 1989.
32. Kalter, p. 22.
33. Ibid.
34. Artlip, pp. 109–110.
35. Ibid. pp. 111–112.
36. Ibid. pp. 191–192.

Chapter 8

1. Neil Kalter, Ph.D., director for the Center for the Child and Family at the University of Michigan, Ann Arbor, personal interview, August 1993.

2. American Psychological Association, press release, August 1991.

3. Robert E. Emery, *Marriage, Divorce and Children's Adjustment* (Newbury Park, Calif.: Sage Publications, 1988), p. 11.

4. Judith S. Wallerstein, Ph.D., founder and executive director of the Center for the Family in Transition, Corte Madera, Calif., personal interview, December 1988.

5. Ibid.

6. Judith S. Wallerstein and Sandra Blakeslee, *Second Chances: Men, Women and Children a Decade After Divorce* (New York: Ticknor & Fields, 1990), p. 298.

7. Kalter, personal interview, August 1993.

8. Wallerstein and Blakeslee, pp. 293–294, 300.

9. Howard Yekell, clinical supervisor of the Open Center, Shrewsbury, N.J., personal interview, August 1993.

10. Ibid.

11. Kalter, personal interview, August 1993.

12. Wallerstein and Blakeslee, p. 60.

13. Kalter, personal interview, August 1993.

14. Wallerstein and Blakeslee, p. 63.

15. Wallerstein, personal interview, June 1989.

16. Kalter, personal interview, August 1993.

17. Wallerstein and Blakeslee, p. 67.

18. Ibid. p. 148.

19. Yekell, personal interview, August 1993.

20. Wallerstein, personal interview, June 1989.

21. Kalter, personal interview, August 1993.

22. Yekell, personal interview, August 1993.

23. Mary Ann Artlip, James A. Artlip, and Earl S. Saltzman, *The New American Family: Tools for Strengthening Step-Families* (Lancaster, Pa.: Starburst Publishers, 1993), p. 161.

24. Kalter, personal interview, August 1993.

Further Reading

If you would like to know more about the effects of divorce on young people and how to cope, the following titles give advice and insight to young adults from disrupted families:

Bienenfeld, Florence. *My Mom and Dad Are Getting a Divorce: For Children, Parents, Teachers and Counselors.* Saint Paul, Minn.: EMC Corp., 1980.

Booher, Dianna Daniels. *Coping . . . When Your Family Falls Apart.* New York: J. Messner, 1979.

Fintushel, Noelle, and Nancy Hillard. *A Grief Out of Season: When Your Parents Divorce in Your Adult Years.* Boston: Little, Brown, 1991.

Francke, Linda Bird. *Growing Up Divorced.* New York: Linden Press/Simon & Schuster, 1983.

Gardner, Richard A. *The Boys and Girls Book About Divorce: With an Introduction for Parents.* New York: Science House, 1970.

Glass, Stuart M. *A Divorce Dictionary: A Book for You and Your Children.* Boston: Little, Brown, 1980.

Krementz, Jill. *How It Feels When Parents Divorce.* New York: Alfred Knopf, 1984.

McGuire, Paula. *Putting It Together: Teenagers Talk About Family Break-Up.* New York: Delacorte Press, 1987.

Mann, Peggy. *My Dad Lives in a Downtown Hotel.* Garden City, N.Y.: Doubleday, 1973. (Novel)

Richards, Arlene, and Irene Willis. *How To Get It Together When Your Parents Are Coming Apart.* New York: David McKay Company, 1976.

Robson, Bonnie. *My Parents Are Divorced, Too: Teenagers Talk About Their Experiences and How They Cope.* New York: Everest House, 1980.

Terkel, Susan Neilberg. *Understanding Child Custody.* New York: Franklin Watts, 1991.

Wallerstein, Judith S., and Joan Berlin Kelly. *Surviving the Break-Up: How Children and Parents Cope with Divorce.* New York: Basic Books, 1980.

If, for some reason, you can't find these books or they aren't right for you, go to your library and look up: *Books to Help Children Cope with Separation and Loss: An Annotated Bibliography* by Joanne E. Bernstein and Masha Kabakow Rudman (New York: R.R. Rowker, 1989). It indexes books by author, title, subject, interest level, and reading level.

Bibliography

Books

Artlip, Mary Ann, James A. Artlip, and Earl S. Saltzman. *The New American Family: Tools for Strengthening Step-Families.* Lancaster, Pa.: Starburst Publishers, 1993.

Einstein, Elizabeth. *The Stepfamily: Living, Loving & Learning.* Boston, Mass.: Shambhala, 1985.

Francke, Linda Bird. *Growing Up Divorced: Helping Your Child.* New York: Linden Press/Simon & Schuster, 1983.

Furstenberg, Frank F., Jr., and Andrew J. Cherlin, *Divided Families: What Happens to Children When Parents Part.* Cambridge, Mass.: Harvard University Press, 1991.

Emery, Robert E. *Marriage, Divorce and Children's Adjustment.* Newbury Park, Calif.: Sage Publications, 1988.

Kalter, Neil. *Growing Up with Divorce: Helping Your Child Avoid Immediate and Later Emotional Problems.* New York: The Free Press, 1990.

LeShan, Eda, *What's Going to Happen to Me?* New York: Four Winds Press, 1978.

Richards, Arlene, and Irene Willis. *How to Get It Together When Your Parents Are Coming Apart.* New York: David McKay Company, 1976.

Wallerstein, Judith S., and Sandra Blakeslee. *Second Chances: Men, Women and Children a Decade After Divorce.* New York: Ticknor & Fields, 1990.

Articles

Brandt, Anthony. "Children of Divorce: From Hurt to Healing." *Parenting,* October 1991, pp. 119, 121, 123, 125.

Clawar, Stanley S. "One House, Two Cars, Three Kids." *Family Advocate,* Fall 1982, pp. 15–17.

Francoeur, Jennifer. "Coping with Divorce." *Vermont Quarterly,* Winter 1993, pp. 19–21.

Hirshey, Gerri. "What Children Wish Their Parents Knew: The Impact of Divorce." *Family Circle,* August 9, 1988, pp. 84–88.

Kantrowitz, Barbara. "Children of the Aftershock." *Newsweek,* February 6, 1989, p. 61.

Kolata, Gina. "The Children of Divorce: Joint Custody Is Found to Offer Little Benefit." *The New York Times,* March 31, 1988.

Levine, Beth. "Children of Divorce." *Seventeen,* January 1990, pp. 95, 110, 111.

Libman, Joan. "Rethinking Joint Custody." *The Los Angeles Times,* May 25, 1988, pp. 1, 4.

Misrach, Myriam Weisang. "The Wicked Stepmother and Other Nasty Myths." *Redbook,* July 1993, pp. 88–91.

Morgan, Leslie. "The Case of the Missing Father." *Seventeen,* January 1991, pp. 92–93.

Neff, David. "Finally, The Truth About Divorce." *Marriage Partnership,* Fall 1989, pp. 35–37.

Rock, Maxine. "Is Divorce Really the Answer?" *Woman's Day,* September 21, 1993, pp. 52–53, 132, 134.

Safran, Claire. "Daddy Buys Me Things You Won't." *Redbook,* October 1993, pp. 130–136.

Satran, Pamela Redmond. "How to Say No to Divorce." *Family Circle*, February 1, 1990, pp. 31–32.

Toufexis, Anastasia. "The Lasting Wounds of Divorce." *Time*, February 6, 1989, p. 61.

Van Biema, David. "Learning to Live with a Past that Failed." *People*, May 29, 1989, pp. 79–92.

Wood, Abigail. "Divorce: It Really Hurts." *Seventeen*, February 1989, p. 30.

Pamphlets

Sixth Circuit Court. *The Friend of the Court Handbook*, Oakland County, Mich.

Index

S

self-esteem, low, 44
separation, 25–26, 35
settlement, 26
sexuality of parents, 75
shame, 18–19
siblings, differing reactions to
  divorce, 7–9, 68
Silvestri, Silvio, 49, 84
Sleeper Syndrome, 87–88
standard of living, 41
stepfamilies, 8–9, 30, 44,
  54–55, 56, 71–82, 91
  benefits, 81–82
  "blended" families, 78–79
  discipline, 80
  halfsiblings, 78
  jealousy of stepparent, 74
  stepsiblings, 77–78, 82
stress, 9, 14, 24, 36, 43, 62, 68
suicide, 38, 61

T

teenagers, 19, 22, 55–56, 63,
  66–68, 69, 80–81

and fathers, 55–56
and parents' sexuality, 75
and peer approval, 67
and rebellion, 66–68
and relationships, 86–88
and stepparents, 73, 75–76
as weapons, 26, 38, 63,
  64–65
Timebomb Effect, 87–88

U

U.S. Bureau of the Census, 27,
  42, 52

V

violence in home, 15, 17
visitation rights, 26, 32, 33

W

Wallerstein, Judith, 10, 36, 41,
  45, 58, 62, 63, 87, 89

Y

Yekell, Howard, 86, 89, 91